A BIT OF A FLAP

Although the Army has been interested in flying since taking to the skies in balloons and giant kites in the late 1800s, people still seemed surprised to hear that the Army flies its own aircraft, even though the present day Army Air Corps has been in existence for more than 50 years. As a Sandhurst cadet I knew little about it myself and followed my father into the Royal Tank Regiment in 1961. Three years later, I caught sight of a poster on the wall calling for volunteers for pilot training. It seemed rather an attractive idea.

In the 1960s, the Army Pilots' Course near the eccentrically-named Hampshire village of Middle Wallop was a remarkably straightforward affair. Having completed the formalities of aircrew medical inspection and aptitude tests at RAF Biggin Hill, you turned up for interview and then reported to the Quartermaster who issued you with all the flying kit you would need. For some reason, this included a beautiful set of Biggles-style goggles which few of us ever got the chance to wear when airborne but which worked a treat on a motorbike.

The *pièce de résistance* was the Mark 1 flying helmet, known locally as the bone-dome. This was in two parts: a fabric inner cap, with built-in earphones, and an outer shell. The ensemble was completed by a foam rubber oxygen mask with built-in microphone.

By the time I reported to Middle Wallop, my total flying experience was as a passenger in a Dragon Rapide to Guernsey, a DC3 back again, an RAF Britannia to Northern Ireland and a howling, vibrating Sycamore helicopter across Salisbury Plain as a Sandhurst cadet. I had never flown in a light aircraft and wasn't at all sure I would like it much.

Behind the main Officers' Mess building, officer students were accommodated in two rows of huts, which were a great deal more civilised than they looked, probably because each one of us was allocated a batman or batwoman to look after us, wake us in the morning with a cuppa, make the beds and generally spoil us shamelessly. Mine was a Mrs Ruston, or 'Rusty' to her charges, and within a few days life was inconceivable without her.

Wondering if I would really emerge from my course as a qualified Army pilot eleven months later, I doubt if I was the only student to try on all his flying kit in his room on the first evening, looking in the mirror at this young spaceman in his bone-dome and oxygen mask...

Since I understood that the Army specialised in flying *between* the trees rather than over them, oxygen was unlikely to be needed too often but the microphone in the mask was the only means of communicating with the instructor in the back seat of the Chipmunk, to whom we were shortly to be introduced.

With the odd exception, all the Chipmunk instructors were retired Service pilots who, to a callow 23-year-old youth like me, looked positively geriatric. One, a Pole who was not always too easy to understand when airborne, was reputed to have flown for both sides during the war. Mine, Eddie Hewett, seemed to be the oldest of them all, with thin white whisps of hair and a bushy white beard. He had started flying in the RAF between the wars on Hawker Hinds and I took to him at once. Rumour had it that he introduced himself to his new students on the first day of the course with an eye patch and one crutch but thank God on this occasion he was his normal self.

Eddie was softly-spoken, with a twinkle in the eye and a gentlemanly, almost courtly manner. He never rose to the bait when asked about his wartime service, although there were occasions when he would hint that

Dedicated to all those Army officers and NCOs who, suspecting that there may be more to life than simply following the regimental tradition, resolved to try something new by volunteering to fly.

Many of them were warned that leaving the regimental family, even for a few years, would end in tears, so encouragement to succeed in a demanding and potentially unforgiving new environment was in short supply.

Mercifully, most of them ignored such dire threats and carved a new and rewarding career in the air, thereby contributing to the enviable reputation of Army Aviation.

Many failed to graduate as aircrew for one reason or another, some were tragically to lose their lives in accidents or on operations, and the rest of them muddled through somehow.

Most of them made mistakes from time to time and, like me, will count themselves lucky to survive. None of them, I suspect, would have missed it for the world.

Ross Mallock

CONTENTS   Page

1.	A bit of a flap	1
2.	Over the oggin	6
3.	The rogue	11
4.	The woodcutter	16
5.	A short spin	20
6.	The wire that never was	24
7.	The production line	29
8.	Going for a whirl	34
9.	A piece of cake	38
10.	The thin green line	42
11.	Fly it like a fixed wing	48
12.	The wrong seat	52
13.	Black Friday	56
14.	A final farewell	60
15.	Possession is nine-tenths	64
16.	A captive audience	68
17.	Don't frighten the horses	72
18.	A pin in the page	76
19.	The queen of the skies	84
20.	The casualty	88
21.	Under paper	94
22.	The open window	99
23.	The specialist	104
24.	The black hole	109
25.	The undiplomatic bag	114
26.	A long day's night	120
27.	The personal touch	127
28.	The ashes	130

MANY A SLIP

by Ross Mallock
illustrated by Tony Pring

Aviation in itself is not inherently dangerous. But to an even greater degree than the sea, it is terribly unforgiving of any carelessness, incapacity or neglect.

Captain A. G. Lamplugh

If you're faced with a forced landing, fly the thing as far into the crash as possible.

Bob Hoover

My husband always said that what impressed him about the Army Air Corps in the 1960s and 1970s was the way they made it up as they went along.

A fellow wedding guest at the reception

Text © Ross Mallock
Illustrations © Tony Pring

All rights reserved. No part may be reproduced, stored in a retrieval system or transmitted in any form by any means, electronic, mechanical, photo-copying, recording or otherwise without the prior written permission of the copyright holder. This book is sold subject to the condition that it shall not by way of trade or otherwise be lent, re-sold, hired out or otherwise circulated without the publisher's prior consent in any form or cover other than that in which it is published.

ISBN 978-1-4452-1014-8

there was quite a story to tell. On one afternoon when the weather closed in and flying was cancelled, all students were told to report to Eddie for instruction on how to abandon the Chipmunk in an emergency. We gathered round an aircraft in the hangar and he showed us the approved technique of sliding open the canopy, unbuckling the harness, climbing onto the wing root and diving off over the trailing edge. The Senior Pilot was there and I had a suspicion that he and Eddie didn't hit it off too well. As soon as the lesson was over, the Senior Pilot walked off but, before the students had started to follow suit, Eddie said quietly 'Now forget all that. The best way to get out of an aircraft like this is to unfasten your harness, stand up in your seat and perch your bottom on the back of the cockpit. Once there, all you have to do is kick the stick hard forward with your foot and you'll be neatly catapulted into the blue. I've tried it many times and it's never let me down!'

The Chipmunk phase of the course was 60 flying hours long, which gave ample time to fly solo once the magic first unaccompanied circuit had taken place. I suspect I flew solo rather more than my colleagues, because Eddie didn't like to fly for more than 45 minutes at a stretch. Whether he was a martyr to piles I don't know but, if so, sitting strapped down to an unyielding seat parachute must have been agony for him. In any case, as time went by I became more confident and particularly enjoyed aerobatics, which Eddie taught me with gusto, albeit in short bursts.

My enthusiasm for aerobatics developed swiftly after my fist solo spin. There were dark rumours that one of our Chipmunks (I never discovered which) was reluctant to recover from a spin and this apocryphal scare gave the exercise a certain frisson of danger. Eddie would have none of it. 'Go and try a spin,' he would say, 'Enter at five thousand feet and recover after no more than three turns. If you don't like it, come home but only after you've done it successfully.'

Entry at five thousand feet seemed perilously low to me the first time I tried it and I inwardly rehearsed Eddie's abandonment technique carefully, just in case. After a while, though, I found spinning gave me an enormous kick and when I climbed out of the aircraft in dispersal there was a silly grin on my face. I began to think that there might be some hope for me as a pilot after all.

I only hurt Eddie Hewett once and was blissfully unaware of it at the time. He had drummed into me the vital importance of checks, which were taught by rote and practised without reference to any aide memoire. While waiting to fly, time was spent in a parked Chipmunk in the hangar, going through vital actions, chanting them over and over again to commit them to memory. On this occasion, Eddie had told me to go and start up our aircraft, planning to jump into the back seat himself when the engine was warm and ready to go, so that he wouldn't have to sit on his wretched parachute for a moment longer than necessary.

I duly started my checks and got the engine running but must have taken a bit longer than usual because Eddie approached the rear of the aircraft without my knowledge while I was testing 'full and free movement of the flying controls'. Having put on his seat parachute, he raised his foot to step onto the trailing edge of the starboard flap at the very moment that I had reached the 'Check half and full flap' section of my liturgy. His foothold on the flap suddenly falling away, he collapsed on his face in a heap. Alas, his chin was just above the lowered flap when I chanted 'Raise flap' to myself and hauled it back up with a bang, catching him a smart blow on his grizzled jaw and laying him out on the wind-swept concrete for a second time. All this was behind my line of sight, so I had no idea why the ground crewman at the port wingtip dissolved into hysterics, until Eddie plugged himself into the intercom with the words 'Mallock, you very nearly killed me just then! Actually, it really was very funny…'

They say you never forget the instructor who sent you on your first solo. We parted company in July 1964 and Eddie retired soon afterwards. Many years later, I returned to instruct at Middle Wallop myself and ultimately to command the place, where I continued to fly the Chipmunk whenever I had the chance.

I treasured my hours in the 'Chippie' but I will always remember Eddie's gentle introduction to the art of flying. They say he was a bit of a Lothario in his spare time but to me he was a wise, modest and delightful man who started me on a lifelong love affair with aviation.

OVER THE OGGIN

With a new set of wings on my chest and posted from my Pilots' Course to Fallingbostel in Germany, I found myself back in the very barracks which had driven me to volunteer for flying training in the first place. As a young officer in the Royal Tank Regiment, I had served for three years as a tank troop leader and Regimental Signals Officer in Fallingbostel and come to the conclusion that there was more to life than lying in pools of oil under a Centurion tank.

I had subsequently qualified for my wings on what was then a helicopter brand new to the British Army, although very old hat indeed to the Americans. This was the Bell 47-3B1, or Sioux for short. Alas, the Army has a way of catching you unawares, so my posting back to Fallingbostel, albeit to a different regiment, was poetic justice of a sort. It coincided with a widespread scheme to introduce helicopters into armoured regiments and infantry battalions, where they would be operated by their own regimental personnel and commanded directly by the parent regiment. This was a brave new venture which was regarded with great suspicion by the small number of Army Air Corps pilots, who operated at more rarefied levels up the food chain.

The fashionable new Sioux had not yet arrived in Germany and so the Third Royal Tank Regiment was to be equipped with three very second-hand Skeeter helicopters. A short conversion course in Detmold convinced me that this was a uniquely British contraption which seemed to rely for its success on totally inadequate power from an ancient De Havilland engine and a lot of ingenuity from its aircrew and engineers. Its main rotor also revolved in the opposite direction from the Sioux's, which gave the aircraft a wayward tail-wagging habit until it was mastered.

Although I had a Flight Commander, I was appalled to find we had no aircraft at all. Before long, however, I was told to report to an RAF Maintenance Unit at Wroughton in Wiltshire, take delivery of a Skeeter and bring it over to Germany. To someone of my inexperience, this was quite an undertaking. I had little experience of flying solo in Germany and had never flown over the sea. Still, a few days back in England were very welcome and I reported to Wroughton with my flying kit and a bundle of maps to cover the journey home.

I was greeted by a diminutive RAF staff test pilot, who appeared to be a Czech or a Pole. The place was awash with Vulcans, Canberras and Lightnings, which he test flew regularly, but his wrinkled face was heavy with concern as he explained that he had never flown a helicopter before. He had read through the Skeeter Pilots' Notes and managed to get it off the ground successfully and had then proceeded to learn how to fly it by trial and error. The problem, he explained, was that he had no idea if the aircraft was serviceable or not because he didn't know how it should normally perform. He laughed nervously, said he rather disliked the Skeeter and that he was very pleased to see me!

It did not take me long to discover that the little Skeeter's handling was far from satisfactory — the cyclic stick stirred vigorously around the cockpit and the helicopter shook violently from poorly adjusted main rotor blades. Neither of the radios functioned properly and the exhaust made rather expensive noises. I dare say an experienced Skeeter pilot would have found dozens of other defects but these would do for starters.

Taking one defect at a time, we waded through the engineering notes and flew her over and over again until, about a week later, I felt we ought to call it quits and get her home to Germany, where the REME engineers in the Detmold Workshops would be able to straighten things out properly.

A telegram arrived to say that I was to fly to Manston in Kent, where I would be met by an Army aircraft which would escort me across the Channel. Regulations stipulated that single-engined helicopters were not to cross to France on their own and I must admit I rather approved of this at the time. Sure enough, I was met at Manston by an Army Air Corps Flight Commander from Osnabrück, who had flown across in an Auster Mk IX. Apart from being an experienced Army pilot, Mike Somerton-Rayner was an aeronautical engineer who owned his own Auster and he had used his trip to England to stock up on various spare parts which were stuffed in the back of his aircraft, half burying his passenger in the rear-facing seat. I knew Mike by repute, and was destined to know him a great deal better in the years to come, but I was delighted to have someone to escort me who knew the business backwards.

I ought to mention that I had never done any sea survival training or received any instruction in how to operate emergency flotation gear, so Mike showed me how to put on and inflate a Mae West and how to operate the seat-mounted rubber dinghy. He was frightfully upbeat about the whole affair. 'Don't worry about a thing,' he said, 'As soon as you coast out over the water you'll think you can hear a change in the engine note and imagine all sorts of crises but it's only twenty miles or so and I'll keep a eye on you all the way.'

The 'light aircraft corridor' from Dover to Calais was to be flown at no more that 500 feet above sea level to keep away from heavier traffic higher up and I had got one of the radios to work intermittently by smacking it with my left hand every so often. At least, I thought, I would be able to chat to Mike if I had a problem.

On 2 May 1965, there was a layer of sea mist at 500 feet over the Channel, through which it was just possible to catch an occasional glimpse of the white crests on the sea's surface immediately below. Horizontal visibility was about half a mile, so there was no sign of France and, after a couple of minutes, no sign of the cliffs of Dover astern either. In fact, as the minutes dragged on and I buzzed along at about 65 knots, I stationed myself to the right of Mike's Auster and a little behind, secure in the belief that his navigation was better than mine and that he was more likely to find the bit of France we were looking for.

I don't think I have ever concentrated so hard in my life. Trying not to listen to the engine in case it missed a beat, I found my world shrinking into a small globe of white in which Mike and I were suspended, apparently motionless. To take my mind off my predicament, I would occasionally give the radio a violent slap and say something to Mike, to be reassured with a brief answer. I never took my eyes off his aircraft for an instant. I knew that he had recently flown himself and his wife from Malaysia to England in his own Auster, so this little jaunt was nothing to him. To me, it was sheer survival. I knew little about instrument flying and the Skeeter's instrument panel was a primitive affair anyway. After about twenty minutes of formation flying in fog, I began to relax.

That was unwise. Without warning, Mike's Auster suddenly banked violently and climbed steeply away from me. As I wondered if perhaps he was avoiding something I hadn't seen, his voice sounded sharply in my bone-dome: *'And where the hell do you think you're going? Check your horizon!'*

Suddenly on my own, unable to see the horizon and totally disorientated, I happened to look at my instruments for the first time. The artificial horizon showed that I was banked 90 degrees to the right and the altimeter was unwinding towards zero as the air speed swept past 100 knots. At the same time, I saw the surface of the sea very close and vertically tilted over my right shoulder. Rolling level, raising the nose and applying full power, I watched as the sea slipped down below me again with less than 100 feet to go.

We broke into clear weather at Calais and carried on to refuel at Ostend. I was still shaking like a leaf as I got out of my aircraft, with that rather awful metallic taste in the mouth that often accompanies the aftermath of a serious fright.

'That's a lesson to remember,' said my escort, with a smile. 'Disorientation can strike at any time when a visual horizon is lost. But that's one of the best things about flying — you'll always remember that moment with a shudder but if you've learnt from it, it won't happen to you again.'

He's right — it never did.

THE ROGUE

We were meant to have three Skeeter helicopters in the Regiment's Air Troop but initially had to make do with two. This didn't matter much, because to start with there were only two pilots anyway, my boss and me. For some reason, aircraft tail numbers tend to stick in the mind like car number plates and even now, more than forty years later, I can remember XT739 (a very well behaved little aircraft) and 563 (another good 'un) which was to join us later when a third pilot was posted in. XT341, however, which I had brought over from England, was a rogue and it wasn't long before she showed herself in her true colours and for some reason it was always at my expense.

It took us weeks to iron out the imperfections she brought with her from the Maintenance Unit but finally she began to fly straight and true without shaking our teeth out on the process. Although still very wet behind the ears, I was interested to see how the Air Troop of a couple of aircraft with a handful of vehicles and men would be put to work. I didn't have long to wait, because one morning the Commanding Officer himself strolled into the hangar to have a chat. Actually, 'hangar' is a misnomer, as the building on the edge of the Tank Park was an old stable with parking for the aircraft along a narrow passageway, with horseboxes on each side. In fact, the passageway was so narrow that the aircrafts' rotor blades had to be folded before we could put them away for the night. They were stacked like spoons down the middle of the building in whatever order we thought they would be used the following day.

The Commanding Officer was an enthusiastic hockey player, as was I, although I found the Army's habit of playing on tarmac pitches pretty unpleasant. In Fallingbostel, matches were played on the parade square, which had a thin layer of fine gravel on the surface. A fierce lunge for the ball could result in agonising gravel-rash and a long embalming session in the Medical Centre.

The CO had had a bright idea.

'Ross,' he said, 'That square needs to be swept before tomorrow's match or people will get hurt.'

Visions of a young subaltern spending all day swishing a broom about were dispelled by his next suggestion.

'Take one of my helicopters and hover it about for half an hour on the square. That should blow off the worst of the gravel.'

I let the 'my helicopter' bit pass for the moment but wasn't sure how to proceed with this conversation. Helicopters and loose articles of any sort, even bits of gravel, need to be kept as far apart as possible and the thought of spending thirty minutes noisily grit-blasting a precious aircraft was pretty unwelcome. I tried to explain the effect of flying gravel on fabric-covered rotor blades, to say nothing of the little engine ingesting debris as it coughed and spluttered round the square. The CO gave me a look as if to say that clearly here was a young pilot with little moral fibre, and stalked off.

We played the match the following day on the usual skating rink of gravel and I actually scored a goal, tripping and peeling copious amounts of skin from elbows, knees and backside. The Colonel, from the touchline, grinned like a Cheshire Cat and who can blame him?

I felt a certain friendship for Skeeter 341, if only because we had both very nearly ended up in the English Channel on our very first trip together. 341, though, had other ideas. Our nearest Army Air Corps unit was in Verden, a short twenty minutes' flight away, and I was sent there to introduce myself to the wearers of the coveted light blue beret, who supported the activities of the 1st Division and were nominally our advisors in flying matters.

It was a pleasant morning and I met a number of kindred spirits who later became firm friends. However, the time came to return to our comical little stable in Fallingbostel and 341 burst into life after lunch and seemed keen to get going. All went well until we reached 200 feet or so as I climbed out of the Verden site when, with no warning whatever, the engine stopped.

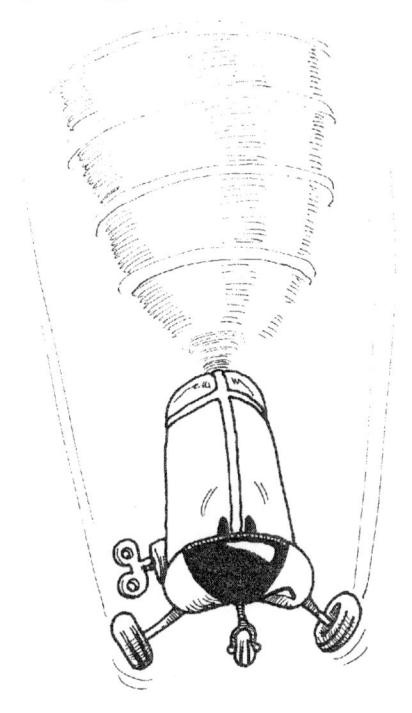

The sudden onset of silence in an airborne Skeeter concentrates the mind wonderfully and I set about an autorotative landing as best I could. Mercifully, 341 and I arrived back where we had started without further excitement and I was surrounded by a small crowd of REME technicians. They seemed rather more interested in the technical cause of my predicament than in my handling of my first real emergency. I thumbed a lift home by road and waited for news of 341's treatment. A couple of days later, they rang to say that they thought it was an ignition problem, that new spark plugs had been fitted and could I come and test fly her before bringing her home.

As I signed for the air test, I recalled the wise advice I had heard during my flying course: always take the technician who had done the work on the aircraft when you test fly it. The REME corporal duly strapped himself in and we took off. Not wishing to tempt fate, I stayed in the hover for a while, listening to the Gypsy Major engine in full song. All appeared in order, so I set off in a gentle climb, only for the engine to fail at exactly the same point. My second engine-off landing was even smoother than the first and as I dismounted the engineers gave me a rather old fashioned look. The corporal who had accompanied me was treated as something of a hero, although I could see that he didn't relish the prospect of a repeat any more than I did.

He need not have worried. A few days later, the call came again. This time, contaminated fuel was suspected, so 341's tanks had been drained and refilled. Would I pop in and do the honours again? This time, the air test went swimmingly and I returned to Verden to offload the brave (and much relieved) technician before setting off for home.

On arrival at Fallingbostel, I hover-taxied across the tank park to the hangar and had just positioned myself outside the doors when the engine quit once more, dumping me unceremoniously on the cobbles. Our own engineers wisely decided to call higher authority and 341 was loaded on a lorry and carted off to the Workshops at Detmold.

We didn't see her again for some time as the manufacturer's representative, a civilian engineer with the most colourful language I had ever heard outside the Services, conducted a thorough investigation. Finally the call came and off I went to Detmold, with a heavy heart.

The Rep explained that he had found the trouble.

'There's a ******* great crack across all four ******* cylinders, which only opens when the engine is ******* hot' he said. 'You're ******* lucky it didn't ******* kill, you, mate!'

My log book shows that I subsequently flew 341 pretty often and with no further alarms. But she had used up four of my nine lives in so many months and wherever I took her I always made sure there was a suitable place within reach to put her down in a hurry — a habit which has stood me in good stead on many occasions since.

THE WOODCUTTER

The three years I had spent in Centurion tanks in Northern Germany had convinced me that they were noisy, smelly and dangerous. Their 27 litre V12 engines gobbled up 4 gallons of petrol per mile across country and had a nasty habit of 'brewing up' — a euphemism for bursting into flames.

Now that I was floating about above them in a helicopter, I could spectate as they brewed up all over the place. Indeed, on one occasion my passenger encouraged me to hover over the top of one such bonfire and try to blow out the flames. Unfortunately, the fierce heat rising from the burning hulk robbed my little Skeeter of both power and lift, and we nearly joined the party.

The lifestyle on exercise in the Air Troop, however, was comparatively civilised. When not flying, there was time to eat, sleep and relax, neither activity having to take place in a hot and smelly tin can. On our first exercise since we formed up, the Troop Commander, Hugo Brooke, wisely took things slowly as we built up experience of living and working in the field. As he made clear, the rest of the Regiment would be looking closely at this new 'kid on the block' and we wanted to show that we knew what we were doing.

The first procedure we practised was simply moving ourselves from place to place. This was not quite as simple as it sounds, since the unvarying principle was that we kept 'one foot on the ground', in other words we never moved about in one bunch. There always had to be one aircraft available for tasking and it needed to have fuel, radios and ground crew to operate it. Our first day was a bit of a shambles and I found it rather hard going. We had selected a couple of ground crew NCOs to act as observers in the aircraft and this made things a little easier. The Skeeter could not be flown 'hands-off' for more than a couple of seconds, so even something simple like folding a map in flight became a gymnastic exercise. My observer, Corporal Cousins, was worth his weight in gold. By the middle of the second day, we had moved half a dozen times with varied success and we stopped for a debrief and a spot of lunch. For some reason, I felt the need to sit down and could not stop myself yawning all the time, despite having had a good night's sleep. This lethargy stayed with me and actually seemed to get worse. I couldn't understand it and tried to get a grip of myself.

Corporal Cousins and I were told to go and find a suitable site for the Troop to move to and off we went. Disregarding all that I had learnt over the year, I rather liked the look of a clearing in the woods in a suitable part of Soltau Training Area, and set myself up for an approach. Cousins had a fairly substantial physique, so with nearly a full tank of fuel the Skeeter had little power in hand. Being half asleep, it never occurred to me to check the amount of power I had available and down we went in a gentle approach, coming to a low hover at the far (upwind) end of the clearing. We then taxied about, discussing where the fuel bowser and command vehicles would go, until we had the site all planned out. We ended up hovering near where I had arrived on our original approach but this time I didn't see some overhanging branches. Mid-yawn, I felt a shudder as the main rotor blades began to scythe their way through the branches of a pine tree and we were enveloped in splintered timber, pine needles and fir cones.

Appalled, I threw the helicopter at the ground and switched off. I dared not meet Corporal Cousins' eye as we cleared the area of bits of timber and pushed the little aircraft away from the trees so that we could take off again. Mercifully, I had the sense to call Hugo and admit what had happened, asking him to come and have a look at my aircraft before we did any more damage. He duly arrived, without an observer, landed nearby and walked across to us. He took in the scene swiftly and then worked his hands along each rotor blade in turn. The Skeeter's blades had a metal main spar, with spruce aerofoil sections over which fabric was stretched, and a thin strip of metal covering the leading edge, which was tacked on with little steel pins. He thought for a moment, then said 'They're a bit battered but should get you to our next position' and he pointed out the spot on the map. Then almost as an afterthought, he asked 'Do you think you'll be able to get out of here?' A very good question...at full throttle, the Skeeter's engine produced 215 BHP which was often inadequate at crucial moments. I hadn't bothered to do an airborne power check before I arrived and was now in the classic predicament of having got into a clearing without the power available to get out again.

Poor old Cousins would have to walk through the forest to some open ground where I could pick him up. He very wisely suggested that I should radio the next position and ask them to send a vehicle to collect him instead. At that stage, anything was preferable to flying with a dozy pilot who chopped down trees.

Overnight, a new set of main rotor blades was delivered and the REME fitted them in time for me to air test the aircraft at first light. I would like to say that I was by then wide awake but I fear this wasn't so. No doubt the change of routine, workload and diet in the field had conspired to exhaust me but I was too ashamed to admit it and soldiered on. A little later, I was taking off from another position on the exercise and Corporal Cousins was alongside me again. This time, as I carried out a concealed take-off, remaining below treetop height, I came just a little bit too close as I turned a corner and heard that familiar 'chop-chop' noise.

'My God, sir!' said Cousins — rather unnecessarily, I thought — '*You've done it again!*'

Indeed I had, but this time the damage was more to what was left of my pride than to the Skeeter.

The other observer in the Air Troop, Corporal Smith, later became a pilot himself, progressing to flying instructor and 'guru' status in the Army Air Corps. I don't think Cousins ever considered flying training after flying with me and I don't blame him one little bit.

A SHORT SPIN

Hugo Brooke, my boss, was a great chap to work for. A gifted aviator and a shrewd officer, he had an impish sense of humour and relished the opportunity to exercise supervision of what was essentially an independent little unit. Although the Air Troop was embedded in the regimental chain of command, there was little day-to-day interference in our activities because people didn't really understand the technicalities of what we did. The nearest professional advice was many miles away near Divisional Headquarters so, as long as we behaved ourselves, we were more or less left to get on with life as we wished.

Out on Soltau Training Area, we were stood down for a day of rest and maintenance before a regimental exercise. We spent the morning practising formation flying in our three Skeeters, unusually all serviceable at the same time. After lunch, we were treated to the stately spectacle of a formation of three cranes flying silently northwards. Suddenly one of them honked to his neighbour and a squaddie was heard to mutter 'Someone's getting a bollocking!'

Later that day, Hugo said that he needed an aircraft for a short trip back to Fallingbostel to collect a piece of test equipment for the REME technicians.

We got on with the business in hand while he was away and, sure enough, we heard the buzz of his Gypsy Major engine later that evening. Being in a non-tactical setting, we had lit a camp fire and were enjoying a beer or two round it. The Troop had moved into the woods, using a long, wide clearing for take-offs and landings, and we were sitting on the edge of the trees watching Hugo as he joined downwind for a wide circuit. Instead of carrying out a normal powered approach, he entered autorotation to simulate an engine failure, floating down along the axis of the clearing and only gently re-engaging the engine during the last few feet. He then hover-taxied back to where we were sitting, to land alongside my aircraft.

While still in the hover, his engine note suddenly rose to a howl and the tail rotor stopped abruptly. All thoughts of beer forgotten for a moment, we watched in horrified silence as the Skeeter, still about four feet from the ground and now with nothing to counteract the braying engine's torque, began to spin to the left with increasing speed. As Hugo's stricken face passed before us for the third time, he lowered the little aircraft onto its wheels with a crunch and slammed the throttle shut. By the time the main rotor had been brought to rest, we had recovered enough for some wag to shout 'How do we score that out of ten, guys?'

Hugo climbed out, we applauded and he acknowledged the applause with a graceful bow. We all gathered round the broken aircraft and congratulated him on surviving what could have been a gruesome tragedy. A lorry and crane were ordered to take the aircraft away the following morning. Hugo and I shared a tent that night and talked about the incident and it was clear that it had upset him. It was some time before I realised why.

To cheer him up, I said how impressed I was with the way he handled the emergency but he brushed this aside.

'It's not quite like that, you know,' he said quietly, 'That was all my bloody silly fault.'

He grabbed a torch and we went out to the aircraft in the dark. We looked closely at the tail cone, through which the tail rotor drive shaft passed. It was bulged half way back where the shaft had broken, presumably distorted by spinning debris.

'There you are,' I said, 'Clearly a mechanical failure which you were lucky to survive because it happened in the hover rather than at height.'

'Have a look at this, though,' said Hugo, as he shone his torch on one of the main rotor blades. About a third of the way out from the hub, it was fractured and swept back by about fifteen degrees. To my amazement, I saw that all three main blades were damaged in the same way.

'I think I know what happened now,' he said, as we returned to our tent.

He had parked the aircraft outside our hangar in Fallingbostel, went inside to collect the test kit and strapped it onto the passenger's seat. The engine was still hot when he started up but before he had the chance to engage the rotors the clutch suddenly failed, slamming all the engine torque into the transmission with a bang. As a rule, this would have stalled the engine and brought the whole affair to a close but on this occasion the hot engine manfully kept going and, although the aircraft slewed round on the ground through ninety degrees, Hugo found that he could open the throttle normally and all seemed well. As he admitted, nobody had seen the incident, it would soon be dark and he had to get back. Perhaps the fact that he hadn't informed Regimental Headquarters that he had left the exercise area had something to do with it.

There was a pause as he took another mouthful of beer.

'Although she flew well enough,' he said, 'There was a strange feeling through the controls and, as I passed the Army Air Corps Flight in Soltau, I considered dropping in and having the aircraft checked out. But our landing site was only a few miles further on and there seemed little point in making a fuss when the Soltau Flight had all gone home.'

Bit by bit, Hugo and I pieced together what had happened. The slam engagement of the clutch had bent the main spar of all three main rotor blades on the ground on start-up at Fallingbostel and had subjected the tail rotor drive shaft to a sudden shock. To the pilot, the only symptom of this was an unbalanced feeling in the controls.

If Hugo had carried out a normal powered approach into the

clearing, the chances were that either he would have lost all or part of a main rotor blade or suffered a tail rotor failure when the shaft fractured with insufficient forward speed to maintain control. As it was, he only re-engaged the engine gently at low level after autorotating into the clearing, so that he was close to the ground when the failure ultimately occurred.

We should have scored him ten out of ten for sheer luck.

THE WIRE THAT NEVER WAS

Of all the hazards which face the pilot of a low-flying aircraft, a wire strike represents the biggest nightmare. It is also probably the most common cause of low flying helicopter accidents. As the old saying goes, there are two types of Army pilot: the one who has hit a wire and the one who's about to.

Well, I'm near enough to my dotage to assume that I'm immune, now that my bone-dome rests gathering dust in the attic. I have had the usual narrow squeaks, of course, particularly in Northern Ireland, where the countryside appears to be held together by a haphazard cat's cradle of wires. One particular incident caused me some difficulty. I was flying a Scout helicopter, conducting what were known as Eagle patrols. These were little more than licensed hooliganism, and I really enjoyed them. A crew of three riflemen would occupy the stripped-out rear of the cabin from which the doors and seat had been removed, sitting on the floor or resting their feet on the skids, attached by a safety strap to a secure point on the Scout's floor. We would blast about at low level, looking for suspicious cars. As soon as one was spotted (and I'm glad to say that I was never invited to justify my suspicions), we would select a field near the road some distance further on, thunder in for a running landing and the crew would dismount at the double, jump over the fence and stop the car. This sport would continue until we got bored with it or actually collared the occupants of a 'hot' car.

On this occasion, I came in very fast but the grass was firm and flat and the Scout's skids were more than man enough for the job. We must have run along the ground for nearly fifty yards before we skidded to a halt, the crew jumped out and I prepared to take off again to give them top cover. For some reason, I looked up and saw out of the corner of my eye a high tension cable stretched right across the spinning main rotor, no more than a couple of feet clear of it. If I had slid any further forward, the tail rotor would have struck it. Spotting the wire was one thing — getting out from under it quite another. As power was applied to take off, the main blades would 'cone up' by a foot or so at the tips, leaving little room to manoeuvre. I did manage to extricate myself in the end but it was in full view of the crew, who had got tired of waiting and came to see what the problem was. They were not too impressed at the way their pilot had behaved and they were dead right.

The worst wire strike I ever suffered never actually happened at all. It was back on dear old Soltau Training Area in Germany in my Skeeter during the latter stages of a regimental attack which took place along an enormous pylon line which stretched for miles along the south eastern edge of the Training Area. The Air Troop had been heavily involved all day, and as our tanks jockeyed about looking for targets, we were popping up from behind the trees looking for the enemy. The problem all day had been that blasted line of pylons. There was no approved method in those days of flying under wires, so to cover the frontage of the regiment we had to climb up one side and dive for cover on the other, inevitably getting spotted and being 'umpired out' in the process.

The exercise ended on a Sunday morning, when German law banned large troop movements, so we had to remain in the field until the following day. The autumn weather was warm and calm with clear visibility, so Hugo Brooke suggested that we each take an aircraft and do some general flying training for a while. My Skeeter had its doors off, I was on my own and the little aircraft was running as sweetly as I could wish. Few Army helicopter pilots these days find themselves in a similar position, since most flying is now done with two pilots. There are few more delicious feelings than knowing that you have a serviceable aircraft, good weather, some spare time and a good excuse to go flying.

I decided to fly up to the north eastern end of the Training Area, which was out of bounds to tanks and therefore unknown countryside to me, and set off at about six o'clock in the evening. After about an hour, I was getting bored of shooting practice approaches into clearings and decided to set off back home.

On the way, I found myself flying along that pylon line again and a totally irrational thought ran through my mind. Those wretched things had been the cause of my nemesis over and over again during the battle and all because I had had to fly over them. Now was my chance to set things to rights. I looked for the highest one I could find — and it was enormous — checked the area around it for any hidden obstacles and (just as important) any spectators and lined up my Skeeter to pass beneath the wires near the pylon. The wires were about eighty feet above the ground and the sensible thing to do would have been to bring the aircraft to the hover by the pylon and taxi quietly under them.

But I wasn't feeling in the least bit sensible. This was going to be fun and I might never get the chance to do it again. Winding the airspeed up to the maximum, I stuffed the nose down and, with the wheels a few feet from the ground, shot underneath at about ninety knots. As I saw them pass over me, I think I might have shouted something like '*Take that, you b...*' but I never finished the sentence. As I looked forward again, there stretched across my flight path was another set of wires even bigger than the ones I had avoided. There were rows of them and avoidance was impossible. With an awful muscular spasm, I plunged through them and waited for the impact before the aircraft disintegrated.

Nothing happened. The Skeeter hummed sweetly on as before. Everything was normal, the controls felt fine; there was no bang or undemanded movement at all. Gently easing into a climb, I gingerly tried a turn to see what had become of those unseen wires.

There was nothing there — just open country and a few small bushes.

Still baffled and frightened, I turned for home and arrived back without incident. After shutting down, I walked round the little aircraft casually examining it for traces of damage from wires. It was untouched.

To my shame, I couldn't face Hugo with the admission that I had behaved in a totally cowboy-like manner when sent off on my own to do some proper training. The fact that I appeared to have seen something which wasn't there, however, ate away at me that evening. Finally I saw our REME Staff Sergeant looking over the aircraft and walked across to join him.

'You alright, sir?' he asked.

'Fine thanks, Staff. Is the aircraft OK?'

'Looks fine to me, but you look awful. What's up?'

I explained as best I could. He heard me out and confirmed that there was no sign of damage that he could see. As we talked about the incident I felt more and more foolish until he suddenly asked 'Where was the sun when this happened?'

'Behind me,' I said. 'It was very low and I didn't want to be dazzled at the critical moment, so I flew down-sun.'

'That's probably the explanation,' he said. 'As you passed under the wires and began to climb the other side, the wires' shadow was thrown onto the Perspex of the canopy in front of you, which probably magnified them too. Must have been bloody terrifying!'

So what I had seen had simply been an optical illusion. I shall never forget that awful moment when I thought my aircraft was going to fly to pieces and all because of my own stupidity.

The angels were not only on my side on that occasion — they arranged for me to be taught a lesson that I was never to forget.

THE PRODUCTION LINE

Germany in the 1960s was full of Skeeter helicopters buzzing about and, as more and more little regimental air troops and platoons sprang up, there were days when the sky was almost dark with them. Occasionally, however, the Skeeter fleet would be infected with some defect or other which spread like a virus across the North German Plain. First, it was fan belts, which would snap for no apparent reason, leading to engine overheating when the cooling fan no longer turned. This was cured by the addition of more belts side by side, so that the odd failure was no longer a crisis.

Next, it was the turn of the exhaust system. The engine was mounted upside down across the fuselage behind and below the cockpit. The exhaust manifold was, in fact, quite close to the ground and the sytem ended in a large curved stove-pipe arrangement. The pipe got very hot and anyone landing on a field with freshly-cut stubble was likely to set fire to the field and, ultimately, to himself and his aircraft if he wasn't careful. The exhaust pipes themselves were prone to cracking and a spate of complaints would come from the local population that red-hot bits of metal were being showered about the countryside. The engineers solved this disease by a clever arrangement of ball-and-socket joints in the exhaust system which allowed it to flex with the vibration without actually snapping off.

But the longest period of unserviceability among the Skeeters was the result of a strange rash of sudden engine failures whose cause was a mystery. Occasionally the engine would cough before it died but the pilot often had no warning of imminent engine failure at all. This was rather bad news and investigations went all the way back to the manufacturer, where it was discovered that the main bearings of some Skeeter engines had been machined to the wrong shape. Once this had been discovered, the enormous task began of calling every Skeeter into the Detmold Workshops for the main bearings to be inspected and, if necessary, changed.

This programme went on for quite a while and a backlog built up of repaired aircraft for which there was no established test pilot. This problem was neatly solved by a long roster of Skeeter pilots who were called to Detmold to test fly the Workshops' output, a week at a time. When my turn came, there were nearly a dozen aircraft lined up outside the hangar, ready to be tested.

It was an almost impossible task. These aircraft had come from all over Germany from units which clearly had very different ideas of what constituted a serviceable helicopter. Some shook my teeth out when I opened the throttle, others suffered from more sedate but still frightening vibrations, while a few were beautifully looked after and a joy to fly. As the week dragged by, one or two aircraft each day would need to be flown a number of times before they could be signed off and returned to their owners.

One in particular simply would not respond to treatment and, as each defect was put right, others would manifest themselves and the whole cycle would be repeated *ad nauseam*. One dank and drizzly day, I had one more trip to do on this little shocker and its heroic technician, one Corporal 'Taff' Jones REME, volunteered to keep me company. I had flown it already three times that day, for no more than ten minutes each time before 'snagging' it again.

After a cursory walk round, we jumped in and fired up the mighty Gypsy Major in-line four cylinder engine. The engine, I knew, was fine;

what we had to do was go and see that the tail rotor was correctly adjusted and with a bit of luck the machine would be signed off as healthy.

The weather was dire but this would only take a few minutes. Taxying onto the runway, I set off towards the east and together Taff Jones and I went through the tail rotor test schedule. All was as it should have been and we congratulated ourselves that at last this aircraft could be sent home serviceable. We were quite low when I called Detmold Tower for a steer to get me home — too low, it seemed, because there was no discernable reply to my call. By this time the cloud base had descended to a few hundred feet in rain and the visibility was poor. Not wishing to climb into the murk, I looked around but was unnerved to realise that I didn't recognise anything familiar about the landscape. No problem — all I had to do was turn back to the west and retrace my steps. The problem was that the tail rotor test had involved a number of turns right and left and I had no idea where we had ended up.

'Do you recognise any of this, Corporal Jones?' I asked, more in hope than expectation.

'No sir,' came the sing-song reply, 'I'm from Fallingbostel, like you.'

All radio calls were in vain but I recalled the map-reading lessons we had had at Middle Wallop. What was it now? Ah yes — when you know where you are, read from map to ground. When you don't, read from ground to map. In other words, find something on the ground and look around the map to see if you can find it.

The map...now where had I put it? In the door pocket of another aircraft, that's where! I had actually come flying without a map of any sort!

There was that slightly metallic taste in the mouth again, as I flew frantically about like a headless chicken. Suddenly, a tractor loomed out of the murk with a drenched farmer at the wheel. Landing next to him, I invited Taff to dismount and ask him in his best German where he thought Detmold was and to point in that direction. This he did, sending me unhappily back the way I had come. Still nothing familiar but miraculously another tractor came in sight. Out got the long-suffering Taff again to repeat the performance. The farmer shrugged his shoulders and swept his arm over a wide arc in the opposite direction. Taff returned to the aircraft and mumbled something about 'a bloody wash-out, if you ask me' as we set off yet again.

It was at this stage that I glanced for the first time at the fuel gauge, which indicated that we were running largely on fresh air. Of course, we hadn't refuelled the aircraft after each short hop that morning and this trip was only to be for a minute or two...

At long last commonsense prevailed and I searched for some sign of human habitation nearby. There was a petrol station by a main road and I hurled the Skeeter at the ground while the engine was still capable of giving a helping hand. As I walked across the road to find a telephone, I noticed a sign naming the village as Helpup. This meant nothing to me but Detmold Tower knew it when I rang. 'Helpup?' they said, 'No problem — we'll get some fuel to you shortly.'

It came in no time — one solitary jerrican of petrol in another Skeeter which was flown, to my great embarrassment, by the instructor who had handled my Skeeter conversion a year or so earlier. To make matters worse, a tour coach drew up and I could hear the guide speaking into his microphone. I could just imagine the spiel: *'Und hier haben wir ein Britischer Dummkopf Hübschrauber Geflieger...'* My misery was complete.

Four and a half gallons of fuel were more than enough to get me the three miles or so back to Detmold but it wasn't enough to cover my embarrassment.

I was to command a regiment in Detmold some fifteen years later and must admit that whenever I drove to Corps Headquarters down the road in Bielefeld I would look at that field opposite the Shell station as I passed through Helpup and shudder.

GOING FOR A WHIRL

Potential flying instructors in all three Services are introduced to the mysteries of teaching people to fly at the RAF's Central Flying School, of which in the 1960s the helicopter branch was at Tern Hill in Shropshire.

If you have read this far, you will wonder what on earth I was doing there. Well, to my amazement I was recommended for training as a flying instructor at the end of my first eighteen months' flying in Germany. All I can say is that there must have been a dire shortage of suitable applicants. On the other hand, perhaps a strange twist of fate can actually straighten out what appears to be an intolerable tangle. In defence of the system which sent me on the course, I can only say that I found the whole instructional scene fascinating and that my time as an instructor led to some of the most delightful and satisfying times in my career.

No roads led to Tern Hill, which was a devilish place to get to and just as difficult to get out of at weekends. This was also the first time I had lived and worked at an RAF station and come into daily contact with pilots from the RAF and Navy. On the whole, they were an entertaining bunch and we got on famously. The course was pretty demanding to a rookie like me because it went so much more deeply into technical detail. Still, if a subject fascinates you, it's extraordinary how your mind can assimilate information which seems at first glance to be beyond comprehension.

The naval students flew the Westland Whirlwind and the RAF and Army the Sioux. By the very nature of their profession, the RAF instructors were pretty mature and experienced operators. To a man, they bewailed the passing of the Westland Sycamore, which had been the standard training helicopter at Tern Hill until the Whirlwind and Sioux arrived.

How anybody could become fond of something like the Sycamore was quite beyond me. The Army Air Corps had flown it when helicopters became a fashionable novelty in the 1950s and I could recall flying in one as a passenger across Salisbury Plain on a Sandhurst exercise. Powered by an Alvis Leonides radial engine buried deep in its guts, it throbbed and vibrated like a thing possessed. In fact it was famous for suffering from a phenomenon called ground resonance, in which, during take-off or landing, it would systematically and violently shake itself to pieces, often before a crowd of admirers who, to a man, would swear never to go near one again.

My Sioux instructor was one of those who viewed the Sycamore through rose-tinted spectacles. One remarkable characteristic as an instructional aircraft was the absence of full dual controls. An instructor's cyclic stick could be fitted in front of the left hand seat but there was no dual collective lever and throttle for the instructor on that side at all. In order to demonstrate a manoeuvre, the instructor had to change hands: his left hand on the cyclic and his right on the student's collective. The mind boggles. Flying a primitive helicopter like the Sycamore was demanding enough without having to do it left-handed.

My instructor, Gordon Mitchell, was a braw Scot and, in common with many of his colleagues at Tern Hill, an expert raconteur. Whenever the weather turned foul, we would congregate in the crew room with mugs of coffee and he would regale us with unlikely flying stories, many of which concerned the dear old Sycamore.

It was winter and one morning we woke to find everything coated in freezing rain. Quite common in other parts of Europe, freezing rain is the result of supercooled water droplets striking a frozen surface and before long everything is coated in a thick layer of tough, clear ice. Even walking about can be hazardous and flying is out of the question. As he peered through the window onto the line of aircraft outside, all encased in a layer of ice, Gordon recalled an incident some years before which involved a rather unpopular Station Commander.

This Station Commander was not, in fact, a flying instructor himself but he strived to compensate for this by flying as often as he could. One winter's day, he reported to the flight line and signed out a Sycamore which stood outside in a row with many others. The problem was the weather — freezing rain and no sign of a thaw. This didn't concern the Group Captain, who prided himself on flying whatever the odds. He would brook no interference. Brushing aside all advice to cancel his flight, he strode out to his aircraft, scraped the ice off the windscreen and clambered in. The instructors, quite naturally, rushed to the window to watch.

The Station Commander brought the engine throbbing to life, carried out preliminary checks and proceeded to engage the ice-laden rotor. The Sycamore had a manual clutch and engaging it required careful co-ordination with the throttle — best done with reference to the tachometer on the instrument panel. Such was his concentration on the job in hand that he failed to notice that the increasing torque from the engine and the mounting speed of the rotor had caused the aircraft to swivel in the opposite direction, thanks to the lack of grip between the wheels and the icy concrete. As he opened the throttle further, the speed of the aircraft's rotation steadily increased, the flailing tail rotor miraculously just missing the aircraft lined up on either side. The instructors watched in awe as he whirled clockwise at gathering speed, still oblivious of his predicament. Finally, the clutch fully engaged and the engine bellowing healthily, he looked out through the frosty windscreen and realised what was happening as the world spun by.

Slamming the throttle shut, disengaging the clutch and hauling manfully on the rotor brake, he hung on like grim death. The fuselage stopped rotating but the inertia in the spinning rotor was such that an even more violent rotation started in the opposite direction as the pilot applied the rotor brake with all his strength. The ashen face of the Station Commander now began to pass by in an anticlockwise direction, again just missing the other parked Sycamores. Eventually, all energy and passion spent, the aircraft came to rest neatly in line where it had started.

There was a pregnant pause, as the instructors grabbed pieces of paper and scribbled scores on them out of ten. These were held up to the window as the pilot's door was opened and a shaken Station Commander emerged, dismounted, saw how he had scored, slipped on the ice and nearly brained himself on the concrete.

Although I didn't know it at the time, I was eventually to command an airfield of my own and, when tempted to push my luck in marginal weather, the vision of the spinning Sycamore always ensured that discretion was the better part of valour.

A PIECE OF CAKE

To my delight (and some surprise) I left the Central Flying School as a qualified helicopter instructor after three months' training. My first job of work was back at Middle Wallop, where my whole chequered flying career had begun.

I was really looking forward to teaching what I myself had learned only two years before. The system, however, was strangely illogical. The training syllabus at Tern Hill was focussed on the art of teaching a student to fly a helicopter for the first time. At the Army Air Corps Centre at Middle Wallop, this crucial duty was undertaken by civilian instructors on the Hiller Mk 12 helicopter — a rather primitive American gadget which had been designed in the early post-war years. These Bristow Helicopter instructors acquired almost legendary status, coming from all sorts of ex-Service backgrounds with thousands of hours' instructional time under their belts.

By the time my unsuspecting first student reached me, he had already spent sixty hours learning the rudiments of helicopter flying on the Hiller and my job was to teach him how to fly the Sioux helicopter in a military role — something for which the instructor's course at Tern

Hill had not prepared me at all.

The whole affair suited me down to the ground. There was very little technical guidance on how to teach the syllabus, I had hardly any military experience to draw on and, in any case, rather looked forward to making things up as I went along. My fellow instructors were a stimulating bunch of individuals, some of them a great deal older than me. One of them, Hugh Colquhoun, had seemed pretty ancient when he took me on a trip on my flying course in 1965, and here I was working alongside him as the fount of all knowledge to some poor unsuspecting student!

To start with, the pace of life was pretty gentle. I was allocated only one student, rather than the usual brace of them, and since he shared his time between flying and ground school during the working day, I only worked for half of it. It was bliss, because the place was full of aircraft of all sorts and I usually entertained myself in a spare Chipmunk on the other half of the day.

If truth be known, I had been secretly rather nervous about the whole affair. Banter in the instructors' crew room indicated that a flying instructor put his life on the line every time the engine was started and I wasn't sure if I would be brave enough to see it through. My first student was an infantry Captain who had distinguished himself in the SAS. Despite his gimlet-like gaze, I liked him and, although he took life more seriously than I did, we got on well.

What was quite extraordinary was the way in which he only had to be told something once. In a nutshell, he never put a foot wrong. As we ploughed on through the syllabus, I began to wonder what all the fuss was about. This instructing lark was a piece of cake: tell him what to do, take off, show him how to do it, let him have a go and come home again. Money for jam, really. Better still, he would occasionally ask me some technical question which baffled me and sent me back to my books to find out the answer. Although I didn't realise it at the time, my student was educating me, rather than the other way round.

It wasn't long before I reckoned he was ready to take the Sioux out on his first solo circuit. As a new kid on the block, I was required to get a more experienced instructor to check him over before sending him off on his own. Suggesting that he get himself a cup of coffee, I went in search of someone suitable and ran into Hugh Colquhoun in the crew room, just stubbing out one of his customary Woodbines. His own student was away solo, so he agreed to take mine for a quick check. I watched them both walk out to the aircraft, start up and set off for the coloured cones in the middle of the airfield which were used as aiming points for approaches.

Since the process was unlikely to take more than fifteen minutes or so, I made myself a cuppa and settled down to watch as they hovered by the cone. They did a steady spot turn to look behind them ('Good lad' I thought) and away they climbed into the circuit. I was absolutely certain that my man was up to it and that Hugh would be impressed with my very first protégé.

After a little while, I began to wonder idly what had become of them. It would normally take about five minutes or so to carry out a sedate circuit and shoot a powered approach to the upwind cone and I was sure that Hugh wouldn't need more than a couple before he was satisfied that my student was ready for his first solo. But there was no sign of them. Ah well, I thought, Hugh has been at this game for many years and knows what he's doing. Perhaps he had decided to go somewhere else to carry out the check.

Forty-five minutes later, I was beginning to think that something ghastly must have happened, when Hugh strode unannounced into the crew room, took off his bone-dome and lit up a Woodbine.

'Well,' he said wearily. 'I sent him off in the end but he needed a lot of help to get it right. He'll be back shortly.'

I couldn't believe it — my student's circuits were usually beautifully flown.

'What was wrong?' I asked, rather nervously.

'Well,' said Hugh, as he inhaled another lungful of smoke from his Woodbine, 'It was all pretty ragged, really. For a start, he cushioned the landing too late and ran onto the ground too fast.'

There followed a catalogue of technicalities, all of which applied not to circuits but to engine-off landings. With a jolt, I suddenly realised where they had been all this time. A separate area of the airfield was set aside for practicing the technique for landing after an engine failure — a demanding exercise only carried out under strict dual control until the very end of the course, when the student might be allowed to do one under his instructor's observation.

I had obviously not made myself clear to Hugh, who assumed that my student was coming to the end of his course and was being checked for solo engine-off landings, rather than for his very first solo circuit. I felt weak at the knees at the thought of what I had done, in stark contrast to my student.

The man himself was full of beans after his adventure. Landing his Sioux neatly outside, he waltzed cheerily into the crew room with a big smile on his face.

'Well done,' I said unsteadily, wondering how I would explain myself.

'Thanks, Ross,' he said. 'That was quite an experience!'

In the circumstances, that must have been the understatement of the year — for both of us.

THE THIN GREEN LINE

My second student was the very antithesis of my first. A happy-go-lucky character with a loud laugh, he had an unhealthy death wish. An hour in a Sioux with this man left me wondering if I would survive until lunch time.

My new Flight Commander was Mike Somerton-Rayner, the man who had saved my life mid-Channel a couple of years earlier, and he saved my life a second time by suggesting that, since I had been instructing at Middle Wallop for all of six months, it was time for a change of scene. The Army had a presence all round the world in those days and apparently there was a shortage of flying instructors. Would I like to go to the United Nations Flight in Cyprus for six months?

Someone else took over my errant student, who subsequently qualified successfully as an Army pilot and is living yet, I believe. My replacement must have been a brave man and a gifted teacher.

I arrived in Cyprus in August 1967 and joined the Flight as its own instructor and the Second-in-Command to its eminent boss, Major David Craig. I had met David briefly at Middle Wallop when I was a student and knew of his reputation then as the ultimate guru of the Army Air Corps fixed wing world. This status was enhanced by an enormous black moustache and a pair of half-moon spectacles. Having reached the pinnacle of fixed wing examiner (or 'Trapper', as such people were rather rudely called), he had converted to helicopters and this appointment was his first in charge of a flight of Sioux.

The UN Flight was based in an old tin hangar on Nicosia Airport, where I shared an office with David. He and the Flight Artificer were the only members who were on a conventional two-year posting, the rest of us serving only for six months in accordance with the UN mandate, which only ran for six months at a time. We got on well and he treated me with a courtesy that my inexperience ill deserved. I discovered later that his conversion to the helicopter world had not been without its problems. Experienced fixed wing pilots of his vintage found the challenges of helicopter flying considerable and he himself had written off a Sioux at Middle Wallop as he taxied away for his first solo sortie, poor fellow.

'I don't really understand these wretched machines,' he would say. 'They don't obey any known laws of aerodynamics whatever. You, Ross,' he continued, 'Will be so kind as to take me on a dual instructional trip every Wednesday morning until further notice.'

So I did. The working day in high summer started at 6.30 and finished after lunch, except for a skeleton duty crew to cover rare emergencies. I rather looked forward to my trips with David, because his problem was more a lack of confidence than anything else. He was perfectly able to land successfully on a promontory in the Kyrenia Mountains — it was just that he doubted his ability to do so. This was a new poser for me as his instructor; he knew what to do but didn't really trust himself to do it. I discovered that the best technique was to keep making reassuring noises so long as nothing unduly dangerous occurred, and sit back with my arms folded — a position which made it quite clear that he was to be master of his own destiny and mine.

It seemed to work and David's flying improved steadily but I did come slightly unstuck on one occasion. David had spent most of his career flying the De Havilland Beaver fixed wing aircraft and old habits die hard. The Beaver had a 'dead' intercom system — in other words, the pilot was not able to talk to his passengers or crew without pushing a switch to the right on the control column, which activated his microphone. By pushing the switch to the left, he could transmit on his selected radio set instead. This led to a delightfully quiet existence in the Beaver's cockpit. The Sioux, on the other hand, had a 'live' arrangement, whereby the intercom was always on. The button on the cyclic stick only needed to be pressed to transmit on the radio. David couldn't get used to this novel arrangement. While flying with me, regulations demanded that he identify himself to Air Traffic Control with my callsign, rather than his own. His opinion of the Cypriot controllers was unprintable and on this occasion he told the Nicosia controller that he was changing to the Approach frequency, only to be answered by a string of information which simply didn't interest him. Pressing his transmit button, he turned to me, flushed with fury.

'Bloody Cypriot air traffickers are worse than useless,' he fumed, 'Worse than in Aden, Malaya, Singapore or Hong Kong. They all ought to be taken out and shot!'

This entire tirade, of course, was broadcast loud and clear across the eastern Mediterranean and no doubt received with horror by the unfortunate controllers themselves. I was in my 'laid-back-arms-folded' configuration at the time and was too late to stop him.

Such excitements apart, life as a United Nations soldier was sweet. The island was divided between Greek and Turkish Cypriot areas, including the city of Nicosia itself, which was divided by what was referred to as the 'Green Line'. The enmity between Greek and Turk was absolute and occasionally would boil over into histrionics. That apart, little ever happened to disrupt our cosy existence, we paid little attention to what was going on elsewhere in the world and we spent most hot afternoons on the beach near Kyrenia, sipping brandy sours between dips in the Mediterranean.

All this changed one autumn morning when David asked me if I would 'pop down to Kophinou' and make contact with the infantry battalion down there.

'There's some sort of flap on, apparently, and the UN has asked for an aircraft to go down there,' he said. 'I expect the CO will want to take a look at his parish from the air or something.'

Kophinou was a village some twenty minutes' flying time south of Nicosia, so off I clattered. It was a warm autumn day, the aircraft's doors were off and I whistled happily to myself. The air was cool and balmy at 3000 feet or so, I knew the route to Kophinou well and I was wondering idly what 'the flap' was all about when I spotted what looked like an armoured car below me, leaving a trail of dust behind it. Suddenly, there were more of them, all tearing across country, with guns and infantry vehicles in support. Could it be an exercise of some sort, and if so whose? I could make no sense of this at all. They were certainly not UN vehicles or weapons and the Greek Cypriot National Guard had no such hardware at their disposal.

The helicopter landing site at Kophinou was a few hundred yards outside the town alongside the main road and consisted of a circle of gravel containing the letter H, surrounded with a ring of white stones. The battalion headquarters, I knew, was in an old schoolhouse on the edge of town. As I climbed out of my aircraft, one of the battalion's riflemen ran past me on his way to the headquarters. He was unarmed and seemed very upset.

'The bastards have taken my rifle!' he shouted, as he swept by. There was a sudden burst of gunfire nearby, and a group of Greek Cypriot National Guard soldiers emerged at the double, followed by an armoured car.

They ignored me, thank heaven, as I secured the main blades of my helicopter, put on my blue UN beret and made my way up the road. It suddenly dawned on me that this was no exercise and that I was now involved in something serious.

It was surreal, really. I had been asked to come and help the battalion without knowing why or how, I had no personal weapon of any sort, my parked helicopter was now in the middle of what looked and sounded like a small battle, and here was I in my shirtsleeves, khaki drill trousers and desert boots, strolling up to the schoolhouse. Bursts of gunfire continued in the distance and there was a sweet, unpleasantly pungent smell which I couldn't identify.

The Operations Room in the schoolhouse had the calm of utter desperation about it. Battalion radio nets could be heard hissing from loudspeakers and the Adjutant stood poring over an enormous map on the table in front of him. Others read messages and scribbled hieroglyphics on wall maps. I cleared my throat and stepped forward.

'Excuse me,' I said, addressing the Adjutant. He didn't even look up.

'Not now,' he snapped, 'The CO's on his way.'

I backed away into a corner and waited. With a crash, the door flew open, the CO, a surprisingly diminutive gentleman covered in dust, burst in and everyone snapped to attention.

'God, this is absolutely hopeless!' he shouted to no-one in particular. 'My riflemen are being disarmed by these bloody people, and they're now in the town murdering every Turkish Cypriot they can find. What the hell are we meant to do?'

'Well, Colonel...' volunteered the Adjutant, but he was cut short.

'If only there was a hill nearby,' the CO went on. 'All I need is a hill that I can climb. I could then look down and see what the hell's going on!'

I couldn't have arranged things better if I had been the scriptwriter. Stepping modestly forward, I cleared my throat.

'Colonel,' I said, 'I've got the next best thing just down the road from here — a helicopter.'

The Colonel paled as he took this in.

'I don't know who you are,' he snarled, 'But if you think I'm going to provoke the National Guard by fluttering about in that...that *thing*...'

He could insult my little aircraft if he wanted to but I wasn't to be denied my rightful place in the battle of Kophinou.

'Sir, you don't have to come with me if you don't want to. I can go up and have a look and let your headquarters know what's happening.'

He was almost shaking with frustration and rage.

'Go away!' he yelled, 'Just go away! And take that contraption with you. *Go home, d'you hear?*'

So I went.

As I took off, the whole chaotic scene was plain to see beneath me. Greek armoured vehicles and tanks were everywhere. Terrified people were running about, trying to escape the carnage, the crackle of gunfire continuing as I headed north for Nicosia.

It was some days before the whole episode was pieced together and I don't think anybody came out of it very well. As it turned out, General

Grivas, the Greek Cypriot leader in exile, had spent some time systematically importing his arsenal over the deserted beaches in the north east of the island, where there had been no UN observation posts. Once he had accumulated his forces, he had swept across Cyprus in his last attempt to claim the island for Greece in what would now no doubt be called an 'ethnic cleansing' operation. He and his army were eventually rounded up and sent packing.

Some years later, when I checked the list of preparatory reading recommended for those selected to attend Staff College, I noticed one erudite book written by that Commanding Officer, who had thereafter become an august General and an authority on operations of that sort.

I couldn't bring myself to read it but that dreadful smell of death and decay will always remain with me.

FLY IT LIKE A FIXED WING

On my return to middle Wallop from Cyprus in early 1968, I resumed my instructional work under Mike Somerton-Rayner, but there was a new gleam in his eye.

'Ross, we're going to form a display team this summer,' he said. 'I need four others to make up the team and we hope to end the season at Farnborough. Are you interested?'

A silly question, really. Here was I, a bachelor with nothing to do but fly all day and enjoy myself in my spare time. The chance of flying in a helicopter display team was not to be missed. As a child I had lived in Fleet, where I was a self-appointed expert in the supersonic research that was going on after the war. My role models (as they would be called these days) had been Neville Duke, Mike Lithgow, Roland Beamont and others, who were rolling back the boundaries of the possible, demonstrating their new aircraft every September nearby at Farnborough and setting speed records in between times.

Mike Somerton-Rayner had obtained authority at Middle Wallop to form a small team of five Sioux. He was to lead it and the rest would be made up of volunteer instructors. It was strictly a spare time activity — we would work normally during the week and set off round the country on Friday evening, returning on Sunday night to start the week's work.

It was to prove exhausting, exhilarating and frightening in almost equal measure.

Mike had a shrewd idea of the routine we would fly, although the details needed to be worked out. Formation flying in helicopters was not an approved exercise in those days, so we had to learn the whole business as best we could. Normal instructional flying started at 8 o'clock sharp during weekdays, so all practice had to be done early in the morning. This was preferable to trying things out at the end of the day, when we were likely to be pretty tired.

The routine which Mike worked out started with the team approaching the crowd in 'echelon starboard' formation — in other words with each aircraft slightly behind and to the right of its neighbour. At the crucial moment, Mike would call for each of us in turn to pull up into what was known as a torque turn: a nearly vertical climb until the airspeed fell off, followed by a smart application of power and a little right pedal. This would spin the little Sioux round 180 degrees until it pointed vertically nose down, from which we would pull out in turn. At least, that was the intention. By doing this one after the other, the display got off to a noisy and spectacular start.

I thought it all looked a bit untidy to start with, and I was in the best position to judge, being 'Tail-end Charlie' — No 5 — who had to coax extra speed from his aircraft in order to stay evenly spaced with the others. It was difficult to standardise the height to which each aircraft climbed and achieve the same rate of rotation at the top.

Early one morning, Mike decided to do something about this. One by one, we were invited to jump into his aircraft so that he could demonstrate what he wanted. Being the last candidate for this treatment, I was able to watch as the Sioux thundered to and fro over the airfield, pulling up into ever more startling torque turns. When my time came, I was astonished at the violence of the manoeuvre as Mike demonstrated it. I knew he was an aircraft engineer but it seemed to me to be little short of cruelty to machinery.

'Don't worry about power at the top of the climb,' he said as he clawed his way to the vertical, 'Just kick it round with pedal as hard as you can. You see?' he enquired as he booted the protesting aircraft round, 'Fly it like just a fixed wing!'

Talking to the others quietly afterwards, I noted that we had each individually come to the conclusion that Mike was welcome to 'fly it like a fixed wing' to his heart's content but we would continue to fly within our own limitations and those of our overworked little helicopters, thank you very much!

Later that week, we set off for the nearby disused airfield at Chilbolton to practice our routine. Mike picked a large ploughed field, told us the display line he wanted to use and where the centre of the crowd would be. The team was at last beginning to get the hang of it and our manoeuvres were looking almost presentable as we ran in for one more practice. We ran in low in 'echelon starboard' and Mike counted us through the opening torque turns. Being at the back of the pack, I could watch the others as they rose and fell and, as I turned myself, I saw No 4, Bill Bailey, begin to pull out of his dive in front of me. As he did so, he turned his head to look over his shoulder at me, now behind him and to his left.

Why he should have done this, I have no idea, but it was a serious mistake. Turning to face the way he was going, he realised too late that the ploughed field was slightly undulating and that he now had insufficient height to pull out safely. We were flying at about 70 knots and I watched in horror as the toe of his left skid dug into the furrow beneath him. His reaction was to try to counteract the sudden nose-down attitude but it was just too late. He pulled the skid out of the plough but the sudden jerk forced the tail rotor into the plough instead. As it broke off, Bill lost all directional control.

Not a word was spoken as he plunged on like a pebble across the surface of a lake, leaving more bits of aircraft in each hole as he bounced along. I should have said something but I was struck dumb, watching in horrified fascination as Bill's aircraft steadily flew apart. Eventually, as momentum was lost, there was little left except Bill in his seat in a Perspex bubble and what remained of the engine behind him. One of the main rotor blades had hit the ground at some stage and had slewed round to join its neighbour on the same side of the rotor mast.

Finally coming to rest, Bill found himself sitting half submerged in a hole with the blades slowly freewheeling on top, giving him a nodding motion as they swept round. By this time the team had tumbled to the fact that all was not well and we had all landed near the wreckage, hoping to be of some help. We all stood round Bill's little hole, unable to do anything because the blades were still rotating slowly and Bill was still nodding rhythmically fore and aft.

I suspect that it was the shock that caused it, but we were all helpless with laughter, including the unfortunate victim. By some miracle, Bill was untouched but he went on rocking for some time as tears poured down our cheeks while we waited for a chance to fish him out.

The only aftermath of the accident that I remember was a call to rename the team the Blue Eagles. Strange as it may seem, we had no official title until then and had got by, tongue-in-cheek, as the Red Rissoles. This had followed a practice formation during a mountain flying session in Wales, when some wag used the term over the radio and it somehow stuck.

Unfortunately, Raymond Baxter spilled the beans during his TV coverage of the Biggin Hill Air Fair and the powers-that-be were very unamused indeed.

A new title was a small price to pay for our survival.

THE WRONG SEAT

As we started the display season in 1968, it's probably true to say that we were actually learning on the job. Because there were only five of us, we had to imagine what our routine would look like when viewed from the ground; we seldom benefited from criticism from the spectator's perspective, which was a chance missed.

Mike Somerton-Rayner, however, was determined that we should have a system which produced smoke, to add dramatic emphasis to what we did. The most obvious way to do this was to mount coloured smoke grenades on the aircraft but this had two drawbacks. Firstly, there had to be a system of firing them from the cockpit at the right time and in the right order and secondly we couldn't turn the smoke off once it had started. It would billow out behind the aircraft until the grenade was exhausted.

Mike had a better idea and manufactured a system to his own design at home. It consisted of a one gallon steel tank, which was strapped onto the radio tray above the engine, from which a small pipe led to the engine exhaust outlet. The tank was filled with diesel fuel and had a

Schrader valve welded onto it so that it could be pressurised by a foot pump. Lastly, a switch was mounted on the pilot's cyclic stick which allowed the pressurised diesel fuel to be injected into the exhaust. It was a remarkably simple and ingenious gadget, which Mike showed me with pride one morning.

'Tell you what,' he said, 'I'll try it out on the ground first and if all goes well you can tell me how it looks in the air.'

Rather typically, he hadn't told anyone else about this little experiment. He wound up the engine of his aircraft, which was parked outside the hangar with all the others, and pressed the switch on the stick. Instantly, a vast and very pleasing cloud of white smoke enveloped his helicopter, prompting the cataclysmic arrival of two fire engines, ready to drown Mike and his aircraft in clouds of foam. I managed to dissuade them from doing so, but it was a close run thing.

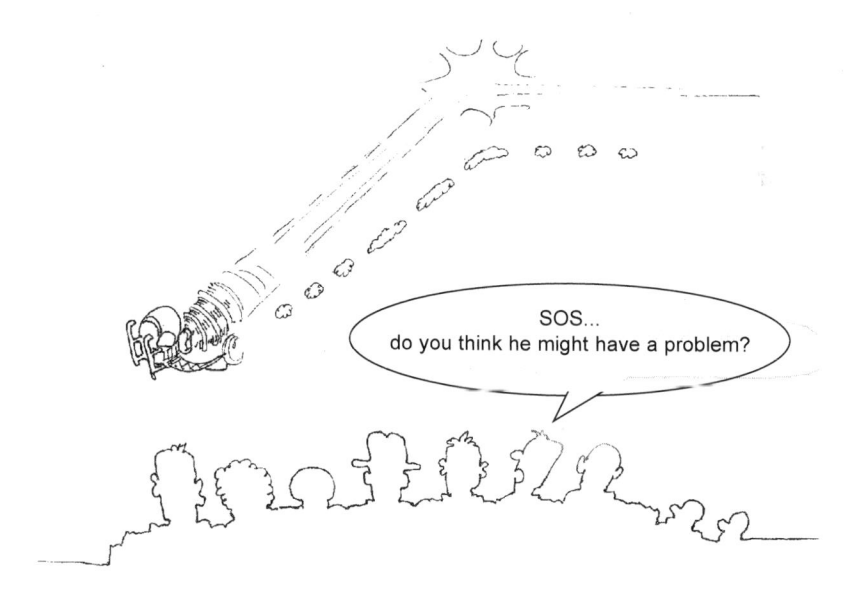

Unfortunately, the system was not quite perfect when he tried it out in flight. The diesel fuel was injected into one of the Sioux's two exhaust pipes but if the power setting was not constant (and it seldom was during a display) the effect was to produce a sort of Morse code in the sky with enormous white dots and dashes and not much in between. We finally settled for a more primitive solution with smoke grenades fired by pulling on pieces of string.

During the season, we often appeared on the same bill as the Red Arrows, whose nine-aircraft formation had started that same year, and it was not long before we thought it would be a good idea to tidy up some aspects of our performance. The Red Arrows were famous for doing everything in formation, including walking out to their aircraft, starting up, taxying, stopping engines and so on. Since we were usually parked much closer to the crowd than they were, we thought a formation landing would be the least we could do.

The problem is that a helicopter landing is a thoroughly unspectacular affair. It is also particularly difficult to do it neatly when four other helicopters are hovering nearby. Suddenly, Mike came up with the extraordinary suggestion that we should line up in the hover and then slam the throttle shut in a simulated engine failure. He would count '3, 2, 1, *go!*' on the radio and on the command 'go' we would close the throttle, kick the aircraft straight and cushion the landing on the concrete using the residual inertia of the main rotor blades.

After our morning display practice, we returned to see a number of students and instructors standing outside their crew room enjoying the sunshine. So here at last was a captive audience for our new formation landing. Lining up alongside each other, we waited for the word 'go' and duly fluttered to the ground together. As he walked past his audience after closing down, Mike asked what they thought of the landing. Not much, it seemed. In fact, they were surprisingly rude about it, saying it was ragged and untidy. As we chatted about it, it became clear that, because our engines were still running, albeit just idling, the fact that we were landing without the use of the engine was not even noticed by fellow helicopter pilots. It was therefore most unlikely to impress the average display spectator.

But Mike wasn't to be put off that easily. 'OK,' he said, 'We'll go the whole hog and turn the engine off altogether. That should grab their attention!'

Now this was a totally different ball game. When the Sioux's engine is shut down in flight, all hydraulic power to the flying controls, except the pedals, is lost and the aircraft reverts to manual control. In other words, the controls instantly stiffen up and become very difficult to move. Since an engine-off landing from the hover demands very precise timing and exact control movements, this becomes a demanding exercise when carried out in your own time, let alone in close formation with four other aircraft.

Mike was unimpressed with this argument, until one of us brought up what seemed to be other insuperable difficulties. The lever used to shut down the engine is on the central console on the pilot's right side. To shut down the engine, the pilot would have to take his hand off the cyclic stick — very unwise when trying to hold a steady hover. If he leant across and used his left hand to shut down the engine, there would not be time for him to grab the collective lever afterwards to cushion the landing in manual control. Game, set and match, we thought.

But no.

'Easy,' said Mike, 'We'll fly from the right seat, so we can all chop the engine with our left hand.' We tried to draw his attention to the passage in Sioux Pilots' Notes which states quite categorically that 'The first pilot's position is the port seat'. Furthermore, the right hand dual stick had no transmit button for the radios and the right hand collective lever no start button for the engine.

Mike swept all dissent aside. 'Don't be silly,' he said, 'Get your bone domes on and we'll go and try it.'

And try it we did. Sitting on the 'wrong' side of the Sioux felt very strange and all sorts of other problems presented themselves for discussion later. The actual manoeuvre was nerve-wracking and we only tried it a couple of times. This time, the audience was enormous, which only made things worse. Their comment was that the whole thing looked like some sort of formation suicide pact.

They were dead right and I'm glad to say it was never tried again.

BLACK FRIDAY

As the prospect of performing at the Farnborough Air Show of 1968 loomed closer, it was decided that the layout of the place did not lend itself to our sort of display. We had concentrated on a routine which exploited the ability of a helicopter to manoeuvre about in a small space. We had displayed at agricultural shows and country exhibitions, where our 'square dance', for example, proved highly popular in an arena. We felt that at Farnborough, with its vast expanse of shimmering concrete and a crowd line more than a mile long, we needed to fly higher and cover more of the sky.

Much time was spent thinking up new things to do, diagrams were scribbled on blackboards and gradually a new routine began to emerge. It was no easy task, because the Sioux, trotting along at 60-70 knots, would take a whole minute just to fly the length of the crowd. We relied heavily on clouds of coloured smoke and the occasional flamboyant 'bomb-burst' to keep the punters happy. The difficulty, though, was always trying to join the formation up again after one of these disruptive manoeuvres, without taking all day about it.

On Friday 13th September, we were practising over Chilbolton Airfield again and trying a new way of joining up which we had gone through on the blackboard early that morning. Two aircraft were meant to approach in line astern from one direction, the remaining three from another, and they were to join up at the top of a short climb. Being 'Tail-end Charlie', I was to be the last to join the party.

To this day I have no idea what went wrong but there was a moment of growing chaos which suddenly snowballed into utter disaster. I recall approaching No 2, who was turning away from me, but closing on him so fast that the bottom of his aircraft suddenly blotted out everything and the noise of his engine was almost as loud as mine. I knew he couldn't see me, so would not take avoiding action, and I was quite incapable of preventing a violent collision. Bringing my aircraft to a shuddering halt at about 200 feet from the ground and banked almost vertically to the right over a small wood, I closed my eyes and hung on like grim death. Against all the odds, we didn't touch and No 2 pounded off into the distance while I tried to recover from a pretty unusual situation. Just as I regained some semblance of control, No 4 suddenly appeared from nowhere and roared over the top of my main rotor. As he passed above me, I felt a sudden shock through the pedals and lost all directional control. He, too, seemed oblivious of what had happened and thundered off to join the other three.

A quick application of left and right pedal established that my tail rotor no longer functioned. It also flashed through my mind that the fashionable theory at the time was that the loss of a Sioux tail rotor was an irrecoverable emergency. A film was going the rounds of flying schools showing a Bell 47 over Sydney losing its tail rotor and spinning down to its destruction in the suburbs below. I had never subscribed to this glimpse of Armageddon and had secretly thought out what my own reaction would be if it ever happened for real.

At this point, I suppose, my short experience as an instructor suddenly took hold of me, because I began chatting to myself as if I was talking a student through actions in an emergency.

'Right, my boy,' I said out loud, 'We've got a problem — we've probably lost our tail rotor. What's the most important thing to do?'

'Keep flying the aircraft,' I replied, 'Reduce power and try to roll level. Look for somewhere to land in a hurry.'

'OK,' I went on, 'We're rolling level now, although we're going very slowly. Anywhere suitable on your side?'

'There's some grass on a bit of a slope but you're going to have to do an engine-off landing, aren't you?'

'That's right, so let's push the nose down to gain a bit of speed, lower the collective fully and close the throttle. Switches and fuel off...that's the ticket...nearly down... watch the slope...check the rate of descent...apply pitch at the last moment, run her on and gently lower the lever.'

We were down. I think I even said 'Well done — not bad at all' or some other patronising comment as I stopped the rotor and undid my harness.

Over the radio, I suddenly heard Mike ask 'Where the hell's Five?' and realised that they were carrying on with their display practice as if

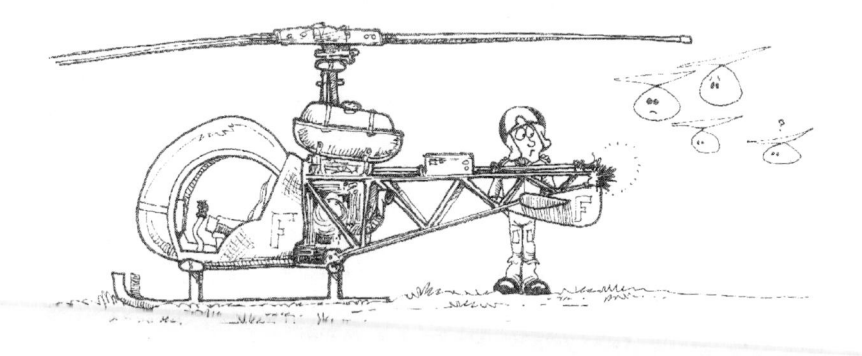

nothing had happened. Feeling rather bruised, I told them where I was and suggested they come and have a look.

The tail rotor and gearbox were missing altogether but miraculously there was no other damage to my helicopter that I could see. I could only gaze in astonishment at the gap which now existed at the end of the tail rotor drive shaft where the gearbox and rotor had been. A search of Number 4's aircraft revealed a tiny dent in the tip of its starboard skid, where it had touched one of my tail rotor blades. Mike suggested that we should call a halt to our activities for the time being and invited me to fly his aircraft back to base while arrangements were made to have mine collected and taken to the Workshops.

Our subsequent display at Farnborough went well and the team reached the end of its first season somewhat battered but unbowed and a great deal the wiser.

There was one extraordinary postscript to this little episode. Two years later, I was lucky enough to command the Blue Eagles, which was by then a full-time job and almost certainly the best one on offer in Army flying. I had taken the team to an agricultural show near Ipswich. The weather was fine and we had a great time giving a couple of displays each day over the weekend.

After our last show, I was walking back to the showground when I was hailed by a farmer who was standing with one foot on the bottom of a five-bar gate. He removed a piece of straw from his mouth, doffed his cap and said 'You fly-boys are stark, staring mad!'

Before I had a chance to reply, he went on: 'And I'll tell you why. I saw two of you hit each other a couple of years ago. I was farming in Hampshire and was sitting on me tractor when you were practising and that. One of you lost his little fan at the back. It spun off into the woods and I went and fished it out later. It's above my mantelpiece now, with a clock in the middle. Looks great, too!'

I had always wondered what had happened to that tail rotor. Now, all these years later, it's nice to think that what might have been a tragic accident actually rewrote our emergency procedures. And it's nicer still that the hardware knocked off my aircraft is now appreciated as an ornament.

A FINAL FAREWELL

Although the Blue Eagles had certainly had their ups and downs (literally) during their first year, our displays had been very well received by the spectators and it was clear that there was a growing audience for more. True, we had had more than our fair share of accidents and incidents during the summer but this was perhaps to be expected. There was, after all, very little experience of this sort of flying since a scratch team of nine Skeeters had been formed especially for the Biggin Hill Air Fair of 1959. They had left no documented advice on how things should be done, leaving us to learn from our own mistakes.

What did surprise and delight me was the news that the team would not only reform for 1969 but that it would become a full time job for the first time. The Ministry of Defence was apparently content for the Army Air Corps to put together proposals to under-implement aircraft and individuals elsewhere in the world to form a small nucleus of a full-time team at Middle Wallop. Subsequent years were even more successful and the torch was enthusiastically handed on in later years.

Mike Somerton-Rayner, the first team leader and the architect of this whole enterprise, spent 1969 preparing for and competing in the London-to-Sydney Air Race in an Auster Mk IX — an almost impossible undertaking by a solo pilot in such a primitive aircraft. He made it to Sydney, against all the odds, but just too late to feature in the official results. Retiring from the Army, he turned his attention to other projects, but we remained firm friends, referring to each other by our original 'Red Rissole' formation numbers. To the bafflement of others, we would address each other this way whenever we met:

'Morning, Rissole One.'

'Hullo, Five.'

When I retired myself, we lived within a few miles of each other and shared a number of interests which kept us in close contact. Mike's passion for flying never left him. He had a collection of ex-Army aircraft which he had bought and renovated, including one of the few Skeeter helicopters on the civil register, and announced his intention to fly solo at the age of 80.

Alas, it was not to be. Indestructible though he had been as a serving soldier, a mild stroke put paid to his ambitions as a pilot. He had been tending a bonfire in his garden when he fell and scorched his knee. As I drove him, clutching ice cubes to his injury, to the A&E Department in Winchester Hospital, there was something about his demeanour which worried me. We chatted away as usual but there was a strangely hunted look on his face which was utterly unlike anything I had seen before.

After the usual wait, we were attended to by the hospital staff and I asked if I could stay with him during the examination. The doctor sorted out his knee and it looked as if Mike was about to be discharged, when I plucked up courage and suggested that there might be something more serious to look into. I couldn't be more specific but mercifully the doctor took the hint and Mike was wheeled off for more tests. It wasn't long before the doctor returned to explain that the patient would be staying for a while longer and that there was no point in my waiting to take him home.

In fact, he never did go home. Subsequent strokes of greater severity put him in intensive care in Southampton, ultimately landing him in a nursing home in Winchester, where I would visit him from time to time. Occasionally, he would show signs of improvement but these were cruelly short-lived and he steadily deteriorated to the point where he could neither move nor speak.

I would visit him every two weeks or so, as would many others. The staff of the nursing home had no idea of his background and assumed that he came from a large family, because he seemed to receive so many visitors. In a manner of speaking, this was true because the Army is a close-knit community, a family of sorts, albeit by another name.

As his condition deteriorated, I found my visits more and more difficult to bear. He would be propped up in his bed, gazing vacantly out of the window onto the garden, surrounded by pictures and messages of support from people all over the world. The television would be on and there was a stack of videos of aircraft, trains and boats which his visitors were encouraged to put on for him, in the hope that he would show some reaction. Having worked with him over the years, and sampled his boundless enthusiasm for madcap projects, I found his growing incapacity heartbreaking. It finally reached the stage where he was unable to react to anything. It seemed that he was unaware of my presence as he gazed unseeing through the window.

Occasionally, I would invite a friend to come with me but this seldom made things any easier. We would end up on opposite sides of the bed and the temptation to chat to each other across Mike's apparently lifeless body was too strong to resist. At other times, I would simply chat to him as if he could hear what I was saying.

Each time I arrived at the front door of the nursing home, I would wonder what good I was doing, spending an hour talking to someone who was, to all intents and purposes, dead to the world.

My final visit was no different from the others. I breezed in with a 'Hullo, Rissole One!' as usual, to which I neither expected nor got a response, then selected a video from his collection and put it into the player. I can't remember now what it was about but after twenty minutes or so I turned it down and started the usual one-sided conversation about life in general and flying in particular.

Finally it was time to go, I stood up and said jokingly, as I always did: 'Fly it like a fixed wing, One.'

As I turned to go, for what turned out to be the last time, he spoke. 'Goodbye, Five.'

He died a few days later.

POSSESSION IS NINE-TENTHS

In September 1969, I found myself at Middle Wallop once again in the Blue Eagles display team, filling in for the last four weeks of the season. This was the culmination of the first full-time season they had flown and it certainly showed. I was coming to the end of an eighteen-month posting in Germany and had been told that I was to command the team the following year.

The aircraft were allocated exclusively to the team, allowing each pilot to take a close interest in his own helicopter, now fitted with an electrically-fired coloured smoke system. Although the leader and his deputy were instructors, the others were selected volunteers from across the Army and competition for a place had been fierce. They had been able to devote all their working days to formation practice and the standard they had achieved was remarkable. Admittedly, the frisson of uncertain excitement we had experienced the previous year was missing but this was perhaps no bad thing!

There were six aircraft and a total of six pilots, allowing each pilot a short period of leave during the summer. A REME Staff Sergeant artificer, a handful of technicians and a couple of drivers completed the assembly with one important addition: a Captain who acted as Team Adjutant, often using the spare aircraft to travel the country organising the team's participation in displays. This freed the team leader from much of the administrative workload, allowing him to concentrate on the Blue Eagles' performance and training.

At the end of the month, personnel began to disperse to their parent units. I returned to Germany until the end of the year, with the delicious prospect of returning in the New Year to form the new team for the 1970 season.

The prospect began to pale within days of my arrival back in England. I was summoned to the Headquarters at Middle Wallop, where a staff officer informed me brusquely that the team would consist of only three aircraft and three pilots. I protested but was told that there was a shortage of suitable aircraft and that three would have to suffice.

'There's no point in getting excited about all this,' he said. 'If you don't like it, we'll find you something else to do.'

It was pretty clear where his priorities lay and display flying wasn't one of them. As I saluted grimly and left his office, a germ of an idea was already forming in my mind.

My merry band of engineers selected the three aircraft we had been allocated and started work while my devious plan began to take shape. Towards the end of 1969, I had heard comments that, with a name like Blue Eagles the team should fly blue aircraft, not brown ones. Whatever plans I hatched, there was no point in going through the 'usual channels' because they would inevitably be clogged by the same staff officer. With the excuse that the team's colour scheme was a matter for decision at the very top, I engineered a short interview with the Brigadier. He thought a two-tone blue scheme, the Army Air Corps' colours, was an excellent idea.

'This is just what we need to keep the Blue Eagles on the map,' he said. 'I'll tell the REME Workshops CO to put all your aircraft through his paint shop. It shouldn't take too long.' The precise number of aircraft was never mentioned.

Try as I might, however, I couldn't visualise a decent display with only three helicopters, particularly since our potential audience was by now accustomed to a five-aircraft routine after our first two seasons. I then remembered that hangar at the RAF Maintenance Unit at Wroughton, where I had picked up that dreadful little Skeeter XT 341 four years before. Fate, for once, played neatly into my hands, because I was told to visit the Wroughton hangar again and pick up a Sioux which belonged to the School of Army Aviation and had just completed a major servicing programme.

Teaming up with an instructor friend, I flew to Wroughton and was disappointed that my Polish test pilot was no longer there. But, as before, there were rows of bright and shiny Army helicopters, waiting for delivery to their units around the world. The foreman was a civilian wearing that trademark brown coat traditionally worn by men of great engineering influence, carrying a clipboard and looking knowledgeable with three pens in the top pocket. I explained that I had come to pick up a Sioux for Middle Wallop. He pointed to one in the row.

'That's yours,' he said, consulting his clipboard. 'If you can give it a quick air test and sign it as serviceable, you can take it with you. I believe the Wallop Workshops will sign the acceptance document when you get back, so your unit can use it the following day.'

A quick trip showed that it was in fine fettle and, as I signed the serviceability log, my airborne chauffeur departed for home.

The chap in the brown coat was in a chatty mood and we talked of this and that while the Sioux was refuelled. He was enormously proud of the work he and his minions did in that hangar but his greatest problem, he said, was a shortage of space.

'Look at all these blinking aircraft,' he said. 'They've all had 'Majors' but can I get their owners to collect them? Can I hell! See those three over there?' He pointed to three Sioux at the end of the line, resplendent in brand new camouflage paint. 'Belong in Hong Kong, they tell me. They're meant to be taken to your Workshops for acceptance but nobody's made any arrangements to pick them up. They've been ready for weeks. All that hard work...'

Suddenly, it all seemed so easy.

'Don't worry about a thing,' I said. 'I'll come back tomorrow with some friends and we'll get them all to the Workshops in one go.'

He was thrilled and offered to have them ready for collection at 8.30 the next morning. My guilt at his gratitude was only matched by my excitement that I might have solved my problem at a stroke. The next day, a bunch of us flew to Wroughton, air tested the three Hong Kong aircraft and flew them to Middle Wallop. On arrival outside the Workshops hangar, I thanked my helpers, went inside and booked all three aircraft into the paint shop without delay.

Within two weeks, six two-tone blue Sioux helicopters were lined up outside my little office at Middle Wallop, I informed the Headquarters that I would need a full complement of five other pilots, and we were in business.

In the real world, someone would have discovered the error and I would have been offered the chance of an interview without coffee with somebody very senior. But it was an unreal world in those days, the team continued flying those six helicopters for more than six years and nothing was ever said.

To this day, I have no idea how they managed in Hong Kong.

Any news of our other aircraft yet, Staff?

A CAPTIVE AUDIENCE

Thanks to days of hard and rather tedious work by our technicians, the Blue Eagles had an almost inexhaustible supply of coloured smoke grenades. Where we got them from I have no idea but crates of the things were locked away in the bomb dump at Middle Wallop. I seem to remember that the supply system applied to each one what would now be described as a 'sell-by date' and the Quartermaster had artfully found some thousands of them reaching the end of their shelf life and purloined them for us.

In their raw state, they were fired by removing a pin and letting go a small handle as they were thrown. Our technicians had replaced the percussion system with an electrical fuse. Each grenade was then loaded carefully into a steel mounting on the aircraft skids and connected to the electrical firing circuit. They were fired in pairs to give a good thick plume of smoke and each pilot could fire three pairs during each display. Our REME Staff Sergeant was the only man in the team who knew how to load them on the aircraft in such a way that the colours blossomed in the right sequence.

Each time we returned from our weekend away, he would load an extra set, which would be fired as we ran in for landing. This proved very popular with the wives and children in the married quarters and became something they looked forward to on a Sunday evening.

There was one very discerning onlooker who never failed to give me an honest opinion of our formation on the run-in. Jimmy, the Officers' Mess barman, had been in situ for as long as anyone could remember. He was very small but always immaculately turned out in black bow tie and starched white monkey jacket. He spoke with a gentle Hampshire burr, having served with the Hampshires during the war, where his hearing had suffered to the point where it was difficult to order a drink without bellowing at the top of one's voice. Jimmy's memory for faces and names was phenomenal. He always seemed to be on duty whenever one turned up in the Mess, often unexpectedly after some years away. Jimmy would be on hand with a cheery greeting, usually using the prefix 'Mr', because the passage of time and the accumulation of rank, however mighty, meant nothing to him. It's no exaggeration to say that it was people like Jimmy who made Service life such a pleasure and provided a certain measure of stability to one's existence.

I never could work out how he did it, but Jimmy never missed the Blue Eagles' return at the end of a weekend's flying. We never warned him that we were on the way and yet there he would be, a tiny white figure standing outside the main entrance to the mess, waiting for our smoke trail to announce our imminent arrival. On a fine evening, I could just make him out from nearly four miles away, like a solitary sentry guarding the front door. He couldn't possibly have heard us coming, even if he had had hearing like a bat.

After putting the aircraft away for the night, I would make my way back to the mess and there would be Jimmy behind the bar, deaf as a post and grinning like a Cheshire Cat.

'I saw you, Mr Mallock,' he would say. 'I saw your Blue Budgies over Porton Down. Not bad — but Budgie 4's landing lamp didn't look straight to me. Now what can I get you?'

Woe betide anyone in the display flying business who thinks he has a captive audience! This was brought home to me towards the end of the 1968 season, when a girl friend decided to sail off to South Africa for twelve months. I knew that she was travelling from Southampton on the *SS Windsor Castle*, and I thought the least I could do was give her a little flypast to wish her *bon voyage*. I dropped a heavy hint that I would bid her farewell from the air.

We had come to the end of the summer display season, the weather was turning cool and damp and our workload as instructors was easing off. I rounded up a couple of friends who seemed happy at the prospect of forming a three-aircraft 'Vic' formation over Southampton Water and off we went.

It was one of those occasions that go wrong so slowly that there is always the hope that things will improve — a typical example of an accident simply waiting to happen. The Sioux was not equipped for instrument flying as it is known today. A very basic cluster of flight instruments was provided for use in dire emergency only, with no navigation instrumentation at all. As we gently entered patchy cloud on our short journey south, my companions began to make mutinous noises over the radio about the whole affair.

Nothing daunted, I ploughed on and before long we entered airspace controlled by Southampton Air Traffic Control. The controller was a Welshman who welcomed me to his tender care with the immortal words 'Must be bloody awful up there, eh, boyo?'

It was indeed bloody awful. My friends were by now hanging grimly onto my vague outline in cloud, hoping I knew where I was going. This was also a problem but my Welsh friend was remarkably co-operative.

'What the hell are you doing, anyway?' he asked.

A very good question which I thought deserved an honest answer.

'We're hoping to meet up with the *Windsor Castle* as she steams down the Sound,' I replied, rather lamely. At this stage, there seemed little point in beating about the bush.

'Well, I'm blowed! I think you may be in luck, too,' came the reply. 'My radar shows something really big heading down towards the Isle of White. Might be what you're looking for. Stay on your present heading.'

At that moment, the cloud dissolved as we burst out into clear weather and there, broadside across our path, was the liner butting through heavy sea. We swept across her bridge in what I hoped looked like a flamboyant farewell to my girl friend.

Anticlimax swiftly followed. My heroic companions turned away, saying that they were happy to make their own way home, thanks awfully, and I didn't blame them.

The passage to South Africa took ten days or so and it was some weeks before a postcard arrived: *A shame that the weather was so foul and that you couldn't see me off. I drank your health in the bar instead.*

As for me, I spent a lot of time talking to Jimmy in the bar that night.

DON'T FRIGHTEN THE HORSES

As a small schoolboy I lived in Fleet shortly after the war and, like many of my contemporaries, became a juvenile authority on high speed flying, much of its research being centred on neighbouring Farnborough. My fascination with flying was heightened by hearing stories told by an uncle who flew fighters off aircraft carriers. He ended up commanding a squadron of Venoms on a carrier which had been fitted with the very latest steam catapult.

Unfortunately, on two occasions the catapult failed when my uncle was attached to it and he and his Venom were flung limply into the sea in front of the ship, which was unable to stop. On both occasions, he had to bump his way along the bottom of the carrier as it sailed over him, finally emerging in its wake. Not surprisingly, he found himself a less stressful job in civilian life.

The expansion of military and civilian aircraft research and development resulted in a procession of accidents, varying from the loss of the Comet airliner from fatigue failure in the Mediterranean to the disintegration of the De Havilland 110 at Farnborough in September 1952. I imagine that most people have a childhood memory that remains sharp in the mind. Mine is as an eleven-year-old, leaning on my bike looking down the Farnborough runway from the high ground to the south west as Derry appeared after aiming his supersonic shockwave at Farnborough from somewhere over the south coast. As he turned steeply to the left away from the runway, the DH 110 fell apart, the cockpit and tailplane crashing into the woods near Cove and one engine crossing the runway and ploughing into the spectators.

Sixteen years later, I was to fly at Farnborough myself, appearing twice with our display team, and on both occasions there was a fatal accident immediately before we were due to fly. Neither impacted anywhere near the public enclosure, thank heaven, and no member of the public has been killed at an air display in the UK since Derry's accident, so strict safety procedures have obviously served their purpose well.

The hours I have spent either flying displays or watching other people do so have given me a useful insight into what is and what is not worth doing in the interests of entertaining the public at air shows. Treating spectators to a spectacle is quite legitimate — in fact it is really the object of the exercise — but frightening them is not.

The Farnborough Air Show of 1968 yielded examples of both. It was the last year in which the Royal Navy would display their fixed wing aircraft, following the decision to hand over their Phantoms and Buccaneers to the RAF. Not surprisingly, the Fleet Air Arm intended to make it a day to remember. This was my first experience of Farnborough as a participant and the scale of the show was beyond belief. The aircrew were treated like royalty and I found myself rubbing shoulders with many of the legendary names in test flying. It was heady stuff.

The Farnborough Air Show in those days was run by the Board of Trade whose officials seemed to relish this moment of glory. Briefings were always introduced by the phrase 'We in the Board of Trade expect...' followed by a catalogue of limitations, one of which was a maximum speed restriction of Mach 0.95. This, in particular, was aimed at the naval participants, who were actually embarked on *HMS Ark Royal* somewhere south of the Isle of Wight, represented at briefings by *Ark Royal's* Lieutenant Commander Flying. The two fixed wing items they flew were very simple: an echelon of four Buccaneers flew by at speed performing a 'twinkle roll' and four Phantoms in a close diamond flew a formation loop. All the aircraft were armed to the teeth.

The Buccaneer was a large and muscular beast and their Red Arrow-style twinkle roll was so out of character with their fully armed state that it took the breath away. The Phantoms, on the other hand, were 'gonged' for speeding on the first day. They ran in very low and just a fraction below the speed of sound but as they pulled up into the loop they accelerated enough to send supersonic shock waves crackling in all directions.

The public loved it but the Board of Trade officials were outraged. Their briefer on the second day emphasised the limitation of Mach 0.95 in a rather hurt voice and the Lieutenant Commander Flying apologised and assured him that he would pass this on to the correct quarter. You could see from his face that it was unlikely to have much effect on the subsequent performance.

Sure enough, as the Phantoms came whipping in from the south west on the final day, a brave press photographer broke ranks and ran out onto the long grass beside the edge of the runway and steadied his camera in preparation for the shot of his life. The Lieutenant Commander sitting beside me said under his breath 'I wouldn't stand there if I were you.' This time the Phantom crews clearly meant to leave their mark in their last appearance in public and the shock wave could be seen flashing across the long grass towards us, ironing it flat in the process. The errant photographer was wearing very wide and floppy trousers and, as the shock wave reached him, his trouser legs wrapped themselves tightly round him as he was lifted bodily from the ground and tossed aside.

The Fleet Air Arm's finale was a different kettle of fish altogether. It consisted of a mass assault by about thirty Wessex helicopters, each with a section of Commandos on board, who then abseiled 200 feet to the ground before attacking an enemy position. The build-up of the helicopters' arrival was spectacular, as the sky seemed to darken with hovering Wessex and the troops whizzed down the ropes onto the grass. As each aircraft disgorged its load, it recovered its rope and moved off.

During the dress rehearsal of the finale, before the public were admitted to the show, I was watching as the helicopters thundered in, dropped their ropes and dispatched their troops to battle. It was certainly the biggest display of its kind I had ever seen and I was watching intently when it occurred to me that all was not well. All the helicopters had recovered their ropes and moved off save one, which remained hovering at 200 feet with the rope dangling beneath it. The section of Marines who had abseiled down were still gathered round the end of the rope looking upwards at the aircraft when, with a blood-curdling shriek, one more Commando leapt out of the helicopter but missed the rope altogether. I watched horrified as he plunged to the ground.

It was, of course, a dummy and the Navy obviously thought it was all terribly funny. Mercifully, commonsense ultimately prevailed and that little stunt was scrubbed from the public version.

The old adage still holds true: entertain the troops by all means but don't frighten the horses.

A PIN IN THE PAGE

With Farnborough Air Show out of the way, the 1970 display season drew to a close at the end of September. The final month had been fun for me because my successor as leader, Tim Taylor, was posted in as my understudy. As we went through each display, Tim sat with me in the cockpit, where he could watch the proceedings and plan how he would do it all in 1971. Coincidentally, he had been at school with me and I had met him again on his flying course some years earlier, after which he had spent most of his flying career in the Far East. After three seasons of display flying, the dreary duty of handing over the team was at least mitigated by leaving it in the care of a close friend like Tim.

I was due to be posted to Germany again in January, but before I left I had the ghastly prospect of sitting the staff/promotion examination in early December. For two dreadful months, I sat alone in my room in the Mess, wending my way through an interminable correspondence course, leading to the examination itself: eight separate papers to be taken over three consecutive days.

Tim and I suddenly realised that we would be at a loose end over

Christmas — the team would have dispersed leaving the aircraft to be prepared for the following year and I would have reduced myself to a gibbering wreck in the examination centre at Bulford, in an attempt to reach the rank of Major and gain a place at Staff College. After some discussion, we hit on the idea of a skiing holiday. I had taken up skiing only five years before and, although Tim's spare time had been spent in the tropics, he was game to give skiing a try. One lunchtime, we found a Services ski catalogue and over a glass of beer we shut our eyes and stuck a pin into one of the pages.

On close examination, the pinhole went through St Anton in Austria. The holiday was sponsored by the Royal Navy and provided accommodation in various buildings near the centre of town, with meals taken in the Rosannastübel, near the level crossing. One original feature of the deal was an overnight train journey from Victoria in what was known as the 'Snow Special'. Two couchettes were accordingly booked and we set off from Andover station to catch our intercontinental express.

As we loaded our luggage onto the train, we spotted the discothèque car at the rear. Things were looking up — with a bit of luck the couchettes would not be necessary if we could only keep ourselves occupied teeny-bopping our way to the Arlberg overnight. As we wended our way to the discothèque, Tim suggested that we needed urgently to draw up a plan. We were unlikely to get very far in 'Snow Special' society as two bachelor Army captains called Tim and Ross. We needed to cook up assumed names and occupations and then see how long we could keep up the pretence with the people we met en route.

All through the summer, we had shared the air display bill with Brian Trubshaw and his prototype Concorde, so I suggested that Tim should be known as Trubshaw — or 'Trubby' to his really close friends. In return, he christened me Peasmold. Occupations were rather more difficult, so we selected the most outrageous ones we could cook up. Trubshaw was the All England Champion Gibbon-throttler, who had been invited to St Anton to rid the forests of rogue gibbons which were swinging through the pine trees and scandalising the tourists. Remembering a recent episode of the TV quiz show *What's my Line*, I elected to be a left-handed straw-whimbler. My cover story was also a corporate invitation from the burgers of St Anton to raise their standard of corn dolly manufacture, which had drastically deteriorated in recent years.

The discothèque car was crammed with people dancing energetically, seemingly oblivious of the way the needle jumped a couple of tracks every time the train went over points but it couldn't have mattered less. To our astonishment, Trubshaw and Peasmold had no trouble whatever in selling their new identities and occupations to total strangers and, as we thundered on through the night, our explanations got longer and more convoluted by the minute. Eventually, hoarse from explaining the technicalities of throttling gibbons and tying corn dollies, we arrived at St Anton station, where we were poured out onto the platform to find our bearings.

We were accommodated in two rooms in a building near the Valluga Hotel, about two hundred yards from the Rosannastübel — an old building ruled with a rod of iron by an elderly Jewish lady called Lilli Stein. For some reason, Lilli took rather a shine to us, although she found my name rather distasteful. She would say 'Ach, I do not like ziss Pissmold!' but this did not curb her habit of serving us complimentary cocktails entitled Rosanna Specials — delightful concoctions with a kick like a mule, which we were convinced were radioactive.

We soon discovered that there were two unattached English girls accommodated in the same building as us. I don't think we ever discovered their names because we only seemed to meet them at breakfast. One was large, gauche and tedious, the other petite, glamorous and talkative. We referred to them as the breakfast girls, subdivided into Boring Breakfast and Sexy Breakfast. The problem was that they appeared to be joined at the hip, so however hard Peasmold or Trubshaw tried to make out with Sexy Breakfast, Boring Breakfast always came too. We gave up trying after a while but Trubshaw did come very close to conquest one evening. We were just returning to our rooms after supper, when we ran into them heading the same way. Gallantly, we offered to see them home and took one each. My luck was out as usual because Trubby flew to Sexy Breakfast's side and together they climbed the front steps to our accommodation. As they walked through the front door, Sexy Breakfast suddenly passed out cold in his arms. After a short debate, it was agreed that Trubshaw ought to carry her to her bedroom to recover, while her tedious colleague indicated the way.

Not wanting to embarrass him, I asked him nonchalantly next morning how things had gone. The disappointment in his voice was palpable as he explained that she was a drama student in London who had clearly been set some homework during the holidays, because she made a miraculous recovery on the landing outside her bedroom and disappeared with a giggle.

Determined to widen our social circle, we noticed that the Ski Club of Great Britain was holding a cocktail party in the Hotel Post in the middle of town. I had had little experience of these affairs but it seemed churlish not to go and see what was on offer, so off we went. It turned out to be a hideous scrum of British tourists, many of them still in ski boots, clutching glasses of sickly glühwein in a seething mass and braying at each other. Just as we were about to write the whole thing off to experience, the door opened and a small posse of people came in, one of whom I had seen before. Racking my brains to work out where I had met that particular girl, I suddenly got it — she had been a disc jockey in the King's Club in St Moritz during a previous holiday with some Army friends. Since I hadn't been able to afford to hang up my anorak on a King's Club peg in those days, I had never seen her in DJ mode but we had met on New Year's Day after I had foolishly accepted a bet that I wouldn't go down the Cresta Run to usher in the New Year. I had made two successful descents out of three attempts and felt rather pleased with myself at six o'clock on that frosty morning and it was nice that she was prepared to witness my first slide down that icy slot. Despite the fact that she hadn't been to bed, she was ravishingly beautiful with a fashionable beehive hairstyle. Captivated though I was, she seemed a little snooty and way beyond my modest means, although I could still recall with a warm glow the way she offered her cheek as I left and said 'Goodbye, love.'

And here she was again in St Anton with her own circle of friends — just as beautiful and, I assumed, just as snooty. Warning Trubshaw that we might have company, I thrust my way through the crush to introduce myself, cringing that I could only remember her surname.

Taking my courage in both hands, I said something trite like 'Hullo — we've met before and your name's Swayne.' She smiled, added that her name was Vivien and said she remembered me from St Moritz. It turned out that she worked as a disc jockey in Annabel's in London (even further from my social circle than ever) but occasionally worked in the Alps in the winter. This year she had got a job in the Valluga Hotel, just round the corner from where Trubby and I were staying. Suddenly, the cooling glühwein didn't taste so awful and a refill seemed in order.

Trubshaw joined us and we were introduced to some of her companions, including a chalet girl called Wiggie. Happily, what had seemed to be a party from hell was turning out rather differently. Furthermore, there was a distinct absence of snootiness all round.

Vivien Swayne was a far better skier than me but seemed content to come with us most afternoons and swore not to blow the secret of our assumed names. Trubshaw and I were doing rather well in that department and established a pattern in the mornings when we skied together. We would separate slightly in the ski lift queue, so that he would get on a double chairlift with a total stranger and I would do the same in the chair behind.

Look! There's one!

@!!

Half way up the mountain, Trubby would make a loud gibbon noise then turn round and shout to me, pointing into the trees, 'See that one, Peasmold?' I would swiftly explain to the stranger next to me what was going on and we would follow Trubshaw's outstretched finger. Invariably, most of the chairlift's occupants would follow suit and the cry would go up 'Yes, there it is! I can see it!' Soon, whole battalions of phantom gibbons could be seen swinging through the forests of the Arlberg and Trubby would make gloating noises about the pleasure he would have in throttling them all later that day.

Skiing with Vivi transformed a mundane holiday into an unforgettable experience. Not only did she ski at great speed but she knew all the pistes and lifts by heart, so we could cover long runs together. Furthermore, she wore very shiny ski pants which meant that whenever she came to grief she would slide for miles, jettisoning skis, sticks, hat and goggles en route. I lost count of the number of times I came round a corner to be faced with all her accoutrements strewn over the snow, with their owner skidding on down the mountain on her burnished bottom.

The heady mixture of romance, exercise and almost constant laughter brought our fortnight to a close all too soon. Vivi, Wiggie, Trubby and I gathered at the Rosanna for one last drink, which turned out to be a marathon, fuelled by Lilli's nuclear Rosanna Specials. By the time we had staggered across the level crossing to the railway platform we were really in no fit state to travel, certainly unable to identify our compartment. It didn't seem to matter much. Trubby and I decanted ourselves onto the train, mumbling that we couldn't read the compartment labels on the windows from the inside. For some reason, this seemed to be very important, so having waved unsteadily to our girlfriends as the train gathered speed, we swung the doors open to inspect the windows from the outside, just as the Snow Special shot into the Arlberg tunnel…

Cold turkey had set in by the time we reached the deserted Mess at Middle Wallop, where everyone was still on leave. With sore heads and dry mouths, we muttered incoherently about a return to St Anton, just to make sure that what had happened had not been a figment of our imagination, when I checked my pigeonhole, stuffed with Christmas mail. Among the cards, some of which addressed me enigmatically as 'Capt G R Mallock AFC AAC' was a letter from the Palace informing me of my appearance on the New Year's Honours List with an Air Force Cross. At that point, little Jimmy the barman put in an appearance and the whole performance started all over again.

By Easter 1971, I was installed as Senior Flying Instructor in Detmold, where I happened to telephone Trubshaw to see what plans he had for leave. St Anton was the obvious venue and I dare say we would each have gone individually, whether accompanied by the other or not. I drove down overnight in my MGB and was so exhausted on arrival at breakfast time that I collapsed onto my bed. My presence, however, was known to the Navy rep through whom we had booked our Easter skiing holiday, who waspishly informed Vivi that I had booked into a double room.

The appearance of Vivi's head round the door confirmed that there was no other girl in the world for Peasmold. Moreover, she had injured her ankle and was unable to ski. Far from curtailing my enjoyment of the holiday, this gave us the chance to be together more than ever. I would ski in the morning and make a plan to meet her at the top of a chair lift. Since she couldn't wear skis, the lift had to be stopped for her at the bottom, so I would watch the top of the lift from a restaurant, knowing that once it had stopped and restarted Vivi would be with me five minutes later. The anticipation was so delicious that I could scarcely contain myself.

By the time I had to leave to return to Germany we were engaged. My drive home in my MG sports car must have taken six or seven hours but I can vividly recall, even now, how my delicious memory of my new fiancée blotted out everything. I didn't even switch on the radio.

Trubshaw was our best man at our June wedding and Wiggie was chief bridesmaid. Before my new wife and I had left the reception, our best man had popped the question to our chief bridesmaid and their engagement was announced as we left on honeymoon.

Peasmold and Trubshaw, who still refer to each other as such, have now been married for more than 35 years, remain in regular contact and their offspring are all close friends. Peasmold is godfather to Trubshaw's eldest son, Trubshaw's wife is godmother to Peasmold's daughter,

Peasmold's son is godfather to Trubshaw's first grandchild and Trubshaw's daughter is godmother to Peasmold's grandson.

And so it goes on — and all thanks to sticking a pin in the page of a skiing catalogue.

THE QUEEN OF THE SKIES

In 1971, at the stage when I was due to convert to the Scout helicopter for the first time, it was going through a very trying time. The Scout was a rare original British design and the first gas turbine helicopter to enter service with the Army. For some reason, the procurement staff had stipulated that it should have a similar rotor diameter to the little Skeeter, although capable of more than twice the payload.

The result was a four-bladed main rotor which whirled round at great speed, causing a substantial downdraught of air and a most satisfactory rasping growl when the Scout was airborne and going about its business. For reasons of design caused by the need to produce a naval variant known as the Wasp, the Rolls Royce Nimbus engine's free turbine at the back had to be harnessed to a tortuous transmission system which turned the main rotor drive through 270 degrees.

Not surprisingly, early development was dogged with technical problems which spurred the Ministry of Defence to buy a dozen French Alouettes off the shelf as a stop-gap measure. Eventually, the Scout settled down and built up an enviable reputation in the Middle and Far East in the 1960s, where she was often referred to as the 'Queen of the Skies'. By the time I came on the scene, however, the Nimbus engine was again beginning to misbehave seriously. In particular, it developed a disconcerting habit of spitting red hot chunks of turbine blade through the side of the engine casing, facing the pilot with the exciting prospect of a landing unencumbered by the engine — something which was an athletic and stirring event both to witness and experience.

The outcome initially was to ban all Scout flying after dark, on instruments, over water, with passengers or at low level. This didn't actually leave much flying to be done except to go up, along and down very gently, after which a technician would thrust a gadget up the exhaust duct to check the state of the turbine blades.

It was all very depressing, particularly for a pilot in the process of learning how to fly it. Furthermore, I was about to return to Germany again, this time as the Senior Flying Instructor based in Detmold, where I would be expected to be the great expert in all things aeronautical, demonstrating manoeuvres and techniques which I had not yet been able to experience myself.

Irritating though this was, it gave me a breathing space to find out what I could about the aircraft and practise what little was permitted. On arrival in Detmold, I was relieved to find a number of old friends there, some of whom were happy to lend me a Scout from time to time. The problem was deciding what to do in it, with all these wretched restrictions in place.

Suddenly, I had a brilliant idea. When learning to fly helicopters on my basic flying course, I had invented a little game which I played whenever I was sent off to practise low speed or hovering manoeuvres. We were taught the mysteries of rotary wing flying on the Hiller Mk 12, a very primitive beast by today's standards but a useful training aircraft which gave rise to the motto: if you can fly a Hiller, you can fly anything. It seemed to take forever to learn to hover the beast but, once this was mastered, further practise could be rather tedious. I would flutter off to one of the old ammunition bunkers which in the 1960s lined the main Andover to Salisbury road. They were about six feet high with very steep, almost vertical grassy sides and it was the sides which gave rise to the entertainment.

The pilot sat in the middle of the bench seat in the Hiller, with space for a passenger on each side. The skids stuck out in front under the fuselage and the tips were easily seen from the pilot's seat. The trick I invented involved landing with the tips of the skids just touching the bottom of the slope, which ensured that the main rotor blades were well clear of the top of the bunker. Then, by carefully balancing the weight of the aircraft between the main rotor and the tips of the skids, it was possible slowly to 'tiptoe' up the slope to the top, rocking the helicopter from side to side as each skid-tip moved upwards. It was enormous fun. Having got to the top successfully, it was an easy matter to tiptoe down to the bottom again. Good, clean fun and it certainly helped to pass the time.

The bunkers had been removed by the time I returned for my Scout conversion at Wallop but, while tootling around Detmold in a Scout, I spotted a similar sort of bunker in the middle of a field. The temptation was too great to resist. Landing at the bottom of the grassy slope, I realised that I could not actually see the tips of the skids, so would have to visualise where they were as best I could. Apart from that, it was as easy as it had been in the Hiller. Furthermore, the fact that the Scout had an automatic throttle and power assisted controls made the game more fun.

After a while, it was time to return home, a short hop of ten miles or so. Happy that I had at last found something unusual to do in a Scout despite all its restrictions, I was perplexed to discover that the aircraft seemed to be very sluggish. The normal cruising speed in a Scout was 100 knots, which would use perhaps 75 per cent of its engine power but this one could barely reach 40 with the engine going flat out. I began to wonder if I was to become another statistic in the Scout's dreary record of shortcomings, when Detmold hove into view and I landed with some relief.

I sought out a REME artificer and explained what the problem was. He sighed and said he would look her over. I felt quite pleased with myself; still very new to the aircraft, I had discovered a new training exercise and had handled a potential technical problem successfully on the way back.

The artificer came into my office half an hour later, holding a Scout pitot tube in his hand. The pitot tube is mounted under the nose where air, entering the hole in the end, is fed to the airspeed indicator dial in the cockpit. He gave me a certain look.

'I think we've found the problem, sir,' he said, holding up the tube. The hole was blocked with earth.

'I don't know where you went this morning.' he went on, 'but you must have been flying bloody low!'

Thank God, he burst out laughing as I explained what I had been up to. Not being able to see the tips of the skids, I had forgotten all about the pitot tube, which I had gaily been grinding into the bunker as I tiptoed up and down. On the way home, the airspeed indicator had been unable to give a proper reading because the pitot tube hole was stuffed with soil. Apart from that, the poor old Scout was fine.

A new tube was fitted and, as far as I know, that artificer never told a soul because I remained in Detmold as the great expert in aeronautics, albeit a very chastened one — and a lucky one too.

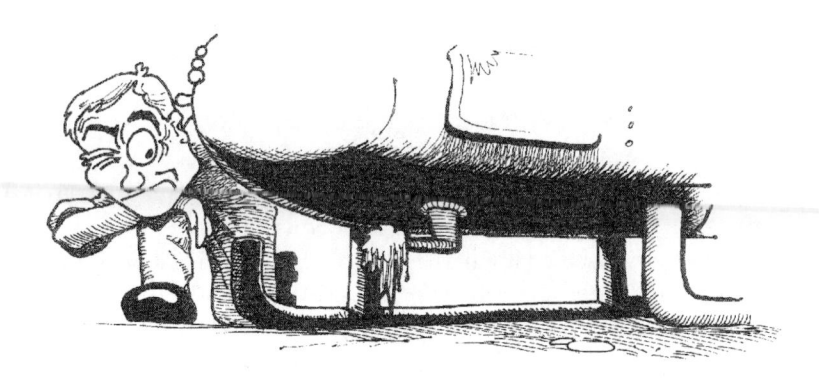

THE CASUALTY

The exigencies of the Cold War in the 1970s never got in the way of the Army's occasional dalliance with show business, particularly in Germany. In particular, there was a strong tradition in Detmold of staging quite a lavish annual air show to raise money for Service charities. Having just arrived from England after my tour as leader of the Blue Eagles, I suppose it was inevitable that Brigadier Dickie Parker, the Army Aviation boss in Germany, should invite me to organise the 1971 Detmold Air Day.

I had never actually organised such a show before but there were plenty of folk about who could help with the technicalities. What I did have, of course, was an address book stuffed with details of people whom I had met on the display circuit in the UK over the previous three years who might like a short trip across the Channel for the weekend. I set about ringing round and before long had accumulated quite a long list of potential participants. Being a good NATO soldier, I also roped in the American Army, German Army Aviation, a crazy Belgian helicopter team and fast jet display pilots from the Second Allied Tactical Air Force. Top of the bill, of course, would be Trubshaw and his Blue Eagles, closely followed by a remarkable part-time Jet Provost team from Lincolnshire called the Poachers, whom I had long admired the previous year.

To provide a contrast to the noisy items on the bill, I included a friend, Roy Legge, who flew an extraordinary aerobatic programme in a historic Bücker Jungmeister biplane, a 'stolen Auster' crazy flying routine by Freeman Smith from Middle Wallop and a finale consisting of a giant, primitive troop-carrying American helicopter which landed in front of the VIP enclosure to disgorge a military band playing our regimental march. In stark contrast to the way these things are organised today, the whole afternoon's display cost us not a penny. Even civilians coming from the UK were prepared to fly for us for the promise of a pleasant duty-free weekend, being put up by my friends locally in their married quarters and enjoying a free dance in the Officers' Mess after the show.

Most of our guest performers arrived on the Thursday afternoon for a rehearsal on Friday, which was an absolute disaster. Why it all went wrong I don't know but I remember Brigadier Parker having very strong words with me afterwards. When Saturday dawned, I had a sickening suspicion that I had bitten off more than I could chew. The only items which had gone according to plan the previous day were the Blue Eagles and Freeman Smith's crazy flying. The others either didn't turn up because of routine commitments elsewhere, or they allowed the prevailing wind to push them over where the crowd was to be — a cardinal sin in flight safety circles. All I could do was brief all concerned about where things had gone awry and hope for the best on the Saturday.

My place on the day was on the balcony of the control tower, where I could hear the radio traffic and try to make sure that the right event took place at the right time. One addition I had inserted into the programme was a starring role for our medical man, an RAMC Corporal from the British Military Hospital in Rinteln, about thirty miles away. He had turned up to provide our only medical crash cover with a Land Rover ambulance. He seemed to me to be a bit thick but terribly keen. Knowing how mind-numbingly boring it can be to hang around all day for an emergency which — God willing — never came,

I suggested that he might like to be involved in Freeman Smith's crazy flying routine.

I had seen Freeman's performance many times and it never palled for me. His Auster would be parked in front of the crowd with a dummy, nicknamed Fred, concealed in the cockpit, equipped with a defective parachute. The commentator would announce to the crowd that the pilot of the Auster was missing and would he please report to his aircraft for his handling display. Freeman, dressed as a member of the public who had clearly enjoyed a liquid lunch, would emerge from the enclosure and weave his way drunkenly towards the aircraft, climb inside and start the engine. Pursued across the grass by a pilot in flying kit, he would taxi away and take off in a heart-stopping lurch. There would follow the most gut-wrenching series of near-disasters as the inebriated spectator tried to control the Auster, each manoeuvre becoming more extreme than the next. Eventually, climbing to a few hundred feet over the centre of the runway, the Auster would tip over onto its side, the dummy would be released to parachute down as the aircraft, now apparently without a pilot, staggered off behind a hill where the Royal Engineers would produce a vast explosion, followed by a mushroom cloud.

It was, I suppose, the aeronautical equivalent of the Benny Hill Show, which I thought would be improved by our medic rushing out to the hapless Fred, hurling him into the back of his ambulance and carting him off with all his sirens shrieking and flashing lights aglow. The RAMC Corporal perked up as I suggested this and we agreed a special site for his ambulance right in the middle of the front row of the crowd, so that his mercy dash would enjoy some dramatic emphasis.

'Whatever you do,' I said, 'Make as much noise as you can — this is your moment!' He nodded enthusiastically.

As often happens after a dreadful dress rehearsal, the show went off very well. I watched the proceedings from the control tower as Roy Legge turned himself inside out in his ancient German aircraft, the Belgian helicopter team gyrated, the Poachers drew hisses of indrawn breath and Trubshaw and his Blue Budgies danced before us.

Freeman Smith's piece of music hall went off without a hitch. There was a gasp of horror from the crowd as the drunken highjacker took off in the Auster, followed by groans of disbelief as the aircraft staggered round the sky, seemingly incapable of flight and yet just missing the ground as it turned itself this way and that. Finally, it rolled over above the runway and Fred departed under his parachute, which failed to open properly, dumping Fred onto the tarmac with a horrible crunch. Our RAMC hero did his stuff gallantly — blue lights flashing and sirens wailing, his Land Rover roared off into the middle of the field, where Fred was lifted from the runway and loaded into the back on a stretcher. Clouds of burnt rubber accompanied the ambulance's departure to a standing ovation.

The only drama that afternoon concerned the solo Lightning fighter from RAF Gütersloh, some twenty-five miles away. He had not been able to take part in the rehearsal because he was on Quick Reaction Alert duty. QRA was a formal operational commitment which demanded that a pair of Lightnings be ready for take-off at a moment's notice to do battle above the East German border, their aircrew primed and ready in their crew-room. The pilot briefed to fly for us was called Bob and I had his telephone number on my clipboard. With ten minutes to go before his appearance, I assumed we would hear his voice on the radio at any moment, asking for the latest time to run in. There was total silence and no response to our calls. With only eight minutes to go, I lost my nerve and rang Bob's telephone extension at Gütersloh.

To my horror, he answered me.

'Hullo Ross, what can I do for you?' he asked.

'Bob,' I said, in rising panic, 'Look, I'm sorry to bother you but you *do* remember that you're meant to be displaying for us here in Detmold in eight minutes' time, don't you?'

'Yeah, sure,' came the reply. 'What's the problem?'

'Well, um...' I wasn't sure what to say.

'Sorry, old bean,' he went on, 'I'm ticking this off as a QRA practice.' The telephone crackled with the sound of Bob gently folding his newspaper and putting it down.

'Don't worry, sport, I'll be appearing from behind the crowd on time in reheat at 1557 precisely — six minutes from now.'

And he did. His cataclysmic routine must have spilt more gin and tonic in the VIP enclosure than the rest of the show put together.

The whole thing went swimmingly, Dickie Parker was content and the dance in the evening was enormous fun.

Sunday was a day off and a chance to tidy up and return Detmold Airfield to its normal state. Trubshaw was staying with us in our married quarter and his wife Wiggie, being an efficient secretary, helped me to type thank-you letters to those who had given us so much of their time.

On Monday morning, having waved goodbye to Trubshaw heading home with his gallant 'Blue Budgies', I was in my office at the airfield, when Freeman Smith walked in.

'My Auster's all ready to go,' he said. 'Thanks for a great weekend but I'd better get back to Wallop. Where's Fred?'

Just then the telephone rang on my desk. It had been red hot all morning and I was expecting another nice message of congratulation on the good show on Saturday. Not a bit of it. The voice at the other end was angry and clearly very senior. It belonged to the Commanding Officer of the hospital at Rinteln, incoherent with rage.

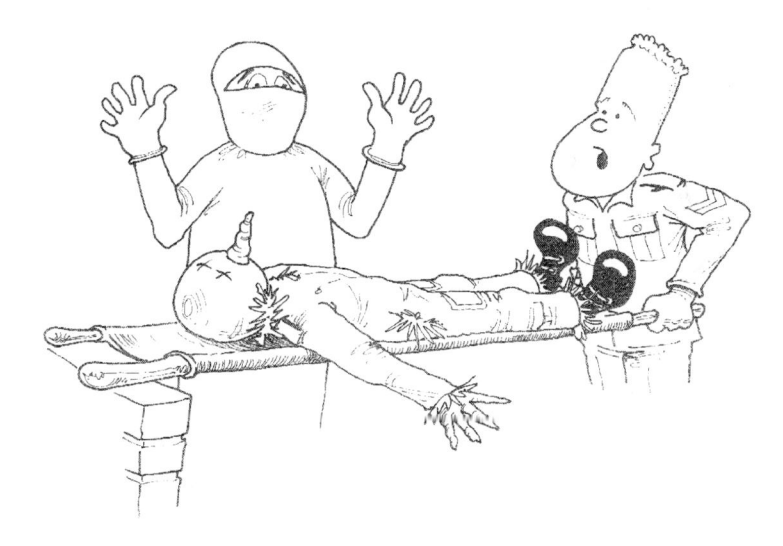

It took me a while to put two and two together and I have to admit that I found it very difficult to keep my voice under control as he gave his account of events on the Saturday afternoon. It had never occurred to me to tell our medic where to go with his precious load in his ambulance but I never thought for a moment that he would treat the occasion as the real thing.

Apparently, having shovelled Fred into the back of his vehicle to the applause of the spectators at Detmold, he had set off with sirens blaring for his hospital's emergency department, where staff had been summoned to save the unfortunate casualty from a fate worse than death.

'Now look here, Major Mallock,' shouted the outraged CO, 'This really isn't in the least bit funny!'

He was absolutely wrong on that score.

UNDER PAPER

Perhaps because I had enjoyed my seven years in Army flying so much, the fifteen-month penance of the Staff College course was a cruel blow. I had never indulged in deskwork if I could help it and the prospect of a flourishing career in the mainstream of the Army held no great appeal. Still, I was lucky to get a place at Camberley and it would have been lunacy to turn down the opportunity to join the rat race, on the basis that the other rats should not necessarily have it all their own way.

I emerged at the other end of the course more convinced than ever that the Army, which prided itself on its ability to 'think the unthinkable' had still not thought hard enough about what aviation could contribute to success. The cold war was the birthplace of cosy military theory — some of it utterly outlandish — but those who came up with fashionable ideas were not faced with the ordeal of proving them in practice, which in retrospect is just as well.

As the course came to an end, I was offered a staff appointment back in the bosom of Middle Wallop — a gentle reminder that I had not excelled as a student of new ideas. Those who were tipped for greatness were placed in appointments in the Ministry of Defence which had little connection with their previous experience — a perverse but effective way of weeding out the inadequate, if only for a lack of versatility.

By this time, I was married with a daughter and another child on the way, occupying our first tiny house in a Hampshire village, and all seemed well with the world apart from my salary, which was laughable. This cosy existence, however, was rudely changed when Greville Edgecombe, our Army Air Corps squadron commander in Hong Kong and someone I had long admired, was suddenly diagnosed with an eyesight problem serious enough to prevent him from flying. The Army Air Corps was so small that the temporary loss of a squadron commander for medical reasons, even on the other side of the world, tended to reverberate round the tribe as people were shuffled about to close the gap.

I was at the end of the chain. Greville was to be replaced by an officer then working in the Ministry of Defence and I was warned that my cosy little staff job at Middle Wallop was to come to an abrupt end, so that I could replace him in the corridors of Whitehall. From now onwards, I was to take the 7.17 train every morning from Andover to Waterloo to fill an appointment known as GSO2 ASD1A in the Main Building of the Ministry.

With a heavy heart, I reached for the 'green book' — a vast plastic-covered green tome which gave the details of every staff appointment in the Ministry of Defence. Heaven knows how it was kept up to date, but each listing gave the name of the current incumbent, his office and telephone details and — most important for me — a brief description of his duties. I scanned the duties of GSO2 ASD1A and my heart sank more deeply still.

'Sponsor of all infantry and army aviation establishments' it ran. This meant that I would be responsible for the quantity and rank of every officer and soldier in every infantry and Army Air Corps unit worldwide, together with their vehicles, aircraft and weapons, in peacetime and in war. It went on: *'Liaison with Military Operations Branch to ensure that units warned for operational duty worldwide are correctly manned*

according to the latest directive from the Chief of the General Staff.' I had no idea what that meant but knew well enough that Military Operations Branch was staffed by the craftiest and most intelligent officers in the Army.

I knew I didn't stand a chance when I read the penultimate line: *'Other routine matters as detailed by the Director of Army Staff Duties.'* Looking towards the front of the green book, I realised that the Director of Army Staff Duties, a Major General, was tipped for greatness and would brook no interference in his bid for stardom, least of all from a rustic young Major who had been transplanted into his organisation at short notice.

I was considering the wisdom of slitting my wrists, when my eyes fell on the final line of the job description: *'Sponsor of the Duke of Edinburgh's Pakistani Army Piping Competition.'*

Now this was more like it! Since music was a passion of mine (although piping was not) this little line in the green book gave me hope that there might be times during my stint in the Ministry when I would be moving in royal circles and perhaps even visiting Pakistan in the course of my new duties.

But even these small diversions were to be denied me. Apparently the Pakistani Army Piping Competition was a result of a royal tour of the subcontinent, when the Duke was so horrified by the dreadful skirl made by the local military pipers that he initiated an annual competition in the hope that it would raise their standard of performance. Every year, therefore, a Scottish pipe major was nominated to visit Pakistan and audition each unit's pipes and drums according to a set list of musical titles. Far from the novelty of visiting Pakistan in the line of duty, my job was to find a suitable pipe major, despatch him to Pakistan and, after careful editing, forward his recommendations to the Palace for the Duke to approve them for publication.

The problem was finding a pipe major who was willing to go. There were not a lot of them at the best of times and most of them had already done at least one stint touring Pakistan, listening with alarm to the enthusiastic ethnic cleansing of their favourite tunes, thereafter swearing that they would never do such a thing again.

Opening the file of previous competitions, I could see their point. *'These pipers play so loudly and so badly that one wonders how anyone can bear to march to their music,'* said one pipe major with feeling. Wrote another: *'The battalion's smartness on parade was quite magnificent until the pipes started, at which point everyone fell out of step.'*

To my great relief, I did eventually find a pipe major who was prepared to travel as adjudicator each year. As he explained to me, it got him out of Scotland for a spell, gave him a change of scene and, despite the noise pollution, he appreciated the enormous enthusiasm of the Pakistanis for the pipes, however inexpert their performance.

On his return from each session overseas, he would telephone me with his impressions. He was a shrewd man with a wonderful sense of humour and I cherished these conversations. I was about to finish my term in the Ministry when he rang me for the last time.

'I realise now' he said, 'That they do everything by ear. In fact, they don't write anything down, either the music or the titles of the pieces they play, which are passed down through the years by word of mouth until they become unrecognisable. This year, I heard a piece which was

One of thame's a snake charmer and the other a piper an' I canna tell which is which!

vaguely familiar but I couldn't identify it. When I asked what it was called, the Pakistani pipe major told me its title was 'Under Paper'. When I jokingly suggested that it must be a march for the Pakistani Ministry of Defence, he became very upset and said that 'Under Paper' was a famous Scottish tune. He was surprised and disappointed that I didn't know it. It was only when I was on the aeroplane coming home that I realised what it was. They had been playing their version of 'A Hundred Pipers.' "

Whether the competition did anything for the standard of piping in that part of the world I have no idea, but it must have raised a laugh in the Palace from time to time.

THE OPEN WINDOW

My two years commanding an Army Air Corps squadron in Netheravon on Salisbury Plain represented some of the happiest and most demanding periods in my life. My squadron was one of four in the regiment, which operated Sioux and Scout Helicopters in Wiltshire, Yorkshire and Essex.

We were largely left to our own devices, so long as we trained according to the guidelines and priorities given to us. There was no knowing when or where we might be expected to serve and detachments were forever rushing off to Kenya, Norway, Cyprus, Northern Ireland or Belize, either on planned deployments or in response to some emergency or other. In the normal course of events, I dislike people looking over my shoulder when I'm busy, so tended to take everyone as far away from base as possible when we trained together as a squadron. The Western Isles, the Isle of Man and even Lundy Island acted as our training bases, which ensured that we were able to get on with our activities without unwelcome visits from senior officers looking for a day away from the office.

I even managed to wangle a trip to Central America myself for a few weeks, claiming that a Squadron Commander couldn't possibly select personnel for service in Belize if he didn't know the layout in that country himself. We operated three Scout helicopters there and, provided you ignored the uncertain history of the single Rolls Royce Nimbus engine which kept you airborne, it was a wonderful place to fly with coastal plains, thick jungle and craggy mountains to choose from. The justification for a British military presence in Belize was based on the unpredictable intentions of the Guatemalans, who occasionally showed signs of aggression across their eastern border with Belize.

How likely it was that Guatemala would wish to invade I don't know but, sure enough, the military planners in the Ministry of Defence suddenly announced that urgent steps were needed to head off another Guatemalan adventure which seemed to be imminent in the summer of 1977. At my lowly level, it was business as usual but the squadron in Colchester was warned to prepare to move to Belize to reinforce our little flight of Scouts. They were picked for the job because their Scouts had been equipped with SS11 anti-tank missiles and the terrain in Belize was such that it was almost impossible to move conventional anti-tank weapons by surface means to where they would be needed.

The first I heard of this business was a message from Regimental Headquarters that the Commanding Officer wished to fly urgently to Colchester to brief the squadron commander on the task which faced him. Usually, if the CO wanted to fly somewhere the Adjutant would ring and ask to borrow an aircraft for the CO to fly himself. On this occasion, the weather was dreadful with low cloud, rain and the threat of thunderstorms. I helpfully suggested that it might be prudent for the CO to go to Colchester by road but this was turned down out of hand.

Before the argument became too heated, the CO turned up in my office with an enormous map under his arm.

'Time is short,' he said, 'And it's vital that I get this map to Colchester without delay. I suggest we fly there together.'

He would brook no argument. A Scout was wheeled out of the hangar and I started some swift flight planning. The forecast was depressing: warm, dank and wet with low cloud across the whole country. The CO turned to me and with a meaningful look and asked innocently whether my Instrument Rating was current — in other words, whether I had completed the minimum hours of instrument flying to allow me to fly about legally in cloud. The regulations concerning instrument flying were specific, as were the CO's expectations that his pilots should have completed all the hours necessary to ensure that they were legally current. Mercifully, a new trial system of low level radar coverage had been established over the south of England, which gave us all ample opportunity to practise our instrument flying procedures. The trial had expanded to the point where it was just possible to remain under radar surveillance from Cornwall to Kent. All that was needed was a chart which showed which airfield provided the advisory service and the radio frequencies on which the service was provided.

The CO knew all this well enough, so there was no escape. I planned a flight from Netheravon to Colchester under the low level radar advisory service and we set off.

We were in cloud almost at once. The Scout's instrument panel, although pretty primitive, could be relied upon to keep things on an even keel, so long as you concentrated hard on the job in hand. There were no navigation aids on board but we were planning to be under radar surveillance the whole way, so would be told what heading to fly to reach our destination.

I was pleased that things seemed to be going rather well. Starting with Boscombe Down, we were identified by each radar controller in turn and, as we reached the boundary of coverage from one radar station, we were transferred to the next.

This was no time for idle conversation with my passenger. The Scout had no stabilised flight control system, so it couldn't be flown without both hands and feet permanently on the controls. Tightening my safety harness, I settled down to the job of keeping the aircraft on an even keel at the right altitude and heading as we thundered on through the murk. We had been going for about half an hour and were somewhere in Oxfordshire, when the CO took his enormous map out of his briefcase and spread it out like a newspaper to look at it. We had not seen the ground since leaving Netheravon, so this seemed a rather pointless exercise to me but a glance at the document showed that it was a highly classified map of the disputed territory in Belize. Enormous red capital letters top and bottom declared that it was SECRET UK EYES ONLY and it was covered in multicoloured lines showing anti-tank engagement areas, proposed unit deployments and nicknames.

The CO had also noticed that the aircraft's windows were steaming up and suggested that we should do something about it. This was a matter of some indifference to me, because there was nothing to be seen outside but it was already warm and clammy in the cockpit and I was reluctant to turn on the windscreen demister, which would have made the environment worse.

'That's fine,' he said, 'I'll open my side window and let a bit of air in.'

This he did by sliding the window open by about half an inch. In no time, the cockpit windows were clear again, although there was nothing to be seen through them.

Suddenly, there was an extraordinary commotion in the cockpit. I had no idea what it was or what had caused it because I was focussed on my instruments but my passenger suddenly shouted 'What's happened? What have you done?'

'I haven't done anything,' I replied, a bit puzzled. 'What's the problem?'

'The map!' he shouted. 'It's gone! Vanished!'

Indeed it had. The 100-knot wind whistling past his partially opened window had sucked the map from his hands and sent it gently gliding down onto the Oxfordshire countryside below, secrets and all.

'We must go after it!' said the CO grimly. 'I'll have you know that map is secret…'

'I know, Colonel,' I said, 'But we are in cloud at a thousand feet and we have no idea what is down there beneath us. We can't just descend in the hope that we'll find the map fluttering about. The ground's down there and we don't know what the cloudbase is.'

'But it's secret!' he spluttered, 'Good God, man, do you know what'll happen when it's found by some passer-by?'

I had a rough idea — compromised secrecy is taken seriously. I liked him and didn't relish the prospect of a new CO, particularly if I had been involved, however bizarrely, in his removal.

There was nothing for it but to admit our predicament to our friendly controller at RAF Benson, who had been handling our transit through his zone. He brought us down from the clouds expertly onto the runway centreline and we clattered off to search for the missing map. It was a hopeless task, since it had almost certainly landed up in some thick woods to the south of the airfield. After a fruitless half hour, we abandoned the search and flew on to Colchester, where I imagine the tactical briefing must have been sketchy without the main evidence to support it.

As it happened, the Guatemalans stayed their hand on that occasion and the Belize garrison was never reinforced from Colchester. If only the aggressors had known what a golden opportunity had been given to them by a Scout helicopter window left slightly ajar!

THE SPECIALIST

Although my helicopter squadron consisted of twelve aircraft, six Scout and six Sioux, I had on my books two more Scouts which were permanently detached to Hereford where they were used by the SAS in their anti-terrorist role. For obvious reasons, this was seldom mentioned in public and in the normal course of events I could ignore them since they were flown by specially-trained aircrew and I only saw the aircraft and pilots when they visited my REME engineers for modification or unscheduled servicing.

Because these aircraft were often tasked to fly at night and in weather which was well below acceptable limits to the rest of us, they were specially modified with a Decca navigation system and a form of autopilot, allowing single-pilot operation under instrument conditions. As far as I am aware, they were unique in this respect and I have to admit that I was curious to know what it was like to fly them.

They remained, however, officially mine, so when I heard that a unilateral decision had been taken to give them a more civilian colour scheme so that their military identity was less conspicuous, I was a bit upset. Their matt green-and-brown was replaced by a glossy battleship grey finish with a tiny ARMY on each side of the tail cone. Bizarrely, they retained their military registration numbers, albeit again in tiny writing. I don't know who was responsible for this new development but it seemed mad to me. Apart from anything else, it ignored the fact that there were aircraft spotters all over the country who seemed to know more about our aircraft than we did, so a new colour scheme would provoke keen interest — the very thing the process was designed to avoid.

I was vindicated when my secret wish to fly one of these special helicopters was granted. The Hereford Flight took pity on me when I asked to borrow one to take part in a squadron exercise in the Western Isles of Scotland. When the exercise was over, we flew back to Netheravon and I opted to take XT 639 myself. I wanted time to get to know all the special gadgets fitted, so I took the long, scenic route and found myself refuelling at Southend. Parking the Scout alongside all the other aircraft near the refuelling point, I noticed an aircraft spotter behind the chain link fence, aiming an enormous telephoto lens at my aircraft. He took a number of pictures and, to be honest, there was really nothing I could do about it. Eventually, he beckoned to me and I walked over to him.

'You're a long way from Hereford,' he said, 'What brings 639 to this neck of the woods? By the way, I like the new colour scheme!'

It wasn't long before they were back to their camouflage paintwork again.

I never did master the navigation system, known as Dectrac, which tuned to a network of Decca radio beacons across the country. It was a bulky affair mounted on the instrument panel with all sorts of needles which shivered and thrashed about all the time. What they were trying to tell me I had no idea.

The automatic stabilisation system, though, was great fun. All it was supposed to do was hold the aircraft at a constant height, heading and speed, allowing the pilot to attend to other matters without the chore of keeping things manually on an even keel. Such things are commonplace now but in those days this was something of a revelation. On one occasion, I had to fly from Chester to Bideford in Devon and XT 639 was again my steed for the day. I can't remember much about the trip, except that I was on my own and it was a glorious summer's day. The beautiful conditions must have lulled me into carelessness, because although I took the trouble to draw a life jacket from the stores for the short sea crossing across the Bristol Channel, I left it on the rear seat. It was only as I was about to leave the Welsh coast that I realised what I had done.

Rather than divert to take the longer route over land, I decided to put the stabilisation system to the test. Settling down to a suitable heading for the north Devon coast at about 1000 feet, I pressed the relevant buttons to engage the system. It did exactly what it said on the tin, so I undid my safety harness and very carefully extricated myself from the pilot's seat and clambered into the rear of the cabin. There, enthroned in the back of the aircraft, I was able to put on my life jacket before returning to the pilot's seat, where I disengaged the system and continued as normal, feeling rather pleased with myself.

Some years later, I mentioned this to a staff officer who had handled and procurement and trials of the Scout stabilisation system.

He was appalled. 'But it was only a simplex system!' he exclaimed. 'If it malfunctioned, which it did regularly, there was no back-up channel to maintain control. If that had happened when you were in the back, you wouldn't have had a chance to regain control before you hit the sea.'

Some time later, I was at Hereford again, this time to help in training new Special Forces personnel to keep cars under observation from the air. This is not actually quite as easy as it sounds and a number of simple but effective techniques had to be mastered to ensure that the target driver was unaware of the presence of the helicopter, yet observation of his car remained uninterrupted.

Special Forces have a habit of using special radios which owe little to the military procurement system and I had to get to know the installation in this particular Scout. The Royal Signals technician responsible for it explained everything, including the rather intriguing induction loop he had fitted in the cockpit which connected the pilot's hearing aid to the radio set. I had never worn a hearing aid before, least of all inside a flying helmet, but it worked a treat, with the added advantage that I could receive radio messages as long as I kept the hearing aid in my ear and remained within twenty yards or so of the parked aircraft. The training day was very long and it was a relief to be able to shut down occasionally for a cup of coffee, lie down in the sun to stretch my legs and still remain informed of what was going on.

The observation exercises with relays of observers demanded surprisingly intense concentration and I didn't realise how tired I was by the middle of the afternoon, when the call came to start up again and go and pick up my next customer. A REME Staff Sergeant was acting as my ground crewman on start-up and it was usual for him to walk in under the spinning rotor to check that the doors were secure and that there were no traces of leaks around the engine. I was busy with my checks as usual, which took rather longer than I was used to because of all the novel equipment installed, and I soon forgot that he was still looking over the engine behind me.

Time was short, so I lifted into the hover. Before I had a chance to move off, however, the aircraft gave a sudden lurch and I glimpsed below me out of the corner of my eye a crouching figure sprinting past my door. The poor man had been standing on the starboard skid to get a good look at the engine, when he had been lifted bodily off the ground.

Thank heaven he had had the presence of mind to leap clear from a height of four feet, because God alone knows what would have happened to him if I had climbed away into the blue. He had the generosity to laugh about it afterwards but I felt sick at the thought of what I might have done to him.

I still do, sometimes, and serve me right!

THE BLACK HOLE

As a squadron commander, I was a great fan of escape and evasion exercises, particularly if I could find some outlandish place to stage them. Escape and evasion seemed to suit the mentality of Army Air Corps soldiers, who were acknowledged as being some of the most intelligent in the Army. To split them into individuals or small groups and task them with moving unseen around the countryside while being threatened with a fate worse than death if spotted, caught and interrogated helped members of the squadron to get to know each other and think for themselves under pressure. These days, such exercises are very seriously regulated and I doubt if anyone can set one up without infringing all manner of Health & Safety regulations.

However, in 1976 I read a newspaper article about Lundy Island, that lump of rock in the middle of the Bristol Channel which had been famous as the hideout of pirates in medieval times. The Island belonged to a Trust which maintained it and let out some of its historic buildings, including the old lighthouse, as holiday accommodation. Lundy was just what I was looking for — a wild and woolly island inaccessible to casual visitors with a small, close-knit population of about thirty people. A visit to the Trust's headquarters in Smith Square clinched the use of Lundy by the squadron over two days in the summer. In return, I was invited to involve the Lundy Islanders in the exercise, on the basis that they would appreciate the chance to do something different.

Three miles long and less than a mile wide, Lundy was too small on its own and I planned to use Bodmin Moor to the south for the second phase of the exercise. In the first, the soldiers were to embark in a landing craft at Ilfracombe in North Devon, and go ashore on a sheltered beach at the southern end of the Island. They would then spread out and make contact with a string of agents who would pass them from hand to hand until they ended up at midnight at the end of the second day near the old lighthouse in the middle of the Island.

The RAF Sea King helicopter conversion unit at St Mawgen had agreed to pick them up that night and ferry them to Bodmin Moor, while dropping hints to the escapers that they were taking them north to Castlemartin in South Wales. I thought this might help to inject a feeling of uncertainty among the escapers and it worked a treat.

In fact, I was so short of spare manpower that I didn't deploy any 'catchers' at this stage but it didn't matter. The escapers were so sure that the Island was infested with them that they treated everybody, even other escapers, as the enemy, which suited me fine.

According to the exercise narrative, the whole country had been the subject of an extremist coup which left the escapers no choice but to contact the underground resistance, christened the Society for the Preservation of the Nation's Genuine Englishmen — or SPONGE for short. The barman of the Lundy Hotel was the first SPONGE agent in the network and he proved a brilliant actor, whispering furtively to each escaper in turn while keeping up a smiling demeanour to all and sundry in his bar.

To my great relief, all escapers made it to the rendezvous at the old light by midnight, as the waves of Sea Kings arrived to scoop them up. By this time, I had flown south to Bodmin Moor, where they were to be dropped off at Davidstow Moor, a derelict RAF airfield. Their first SPONGE agent was upstairs in the shell of the old control tower. There is nothing more derelict than an abandoned airfield and the hulk of the control tower in the moonlight looked like something from a horror film.

    I had arranged for the first contact on the Moor itself to be a female, having managed to persuade a girl who worked in the local pub near Netheravon to fill the role, installing her with a radio set in a small hut at the bottom of the highest promontory on the Moor, Brown Willy. There was precious little contact with women during the working day in the Army in those days, and I thought this would add a veneer of the unusual to the proceedings. Her code name was 'Sponge-bag' and the escapers were briefed to make their way to the summit of Brown Willy, where they would find the component parts of a radio set concealed in the stones of a cairn. They were briefed to assemble the set, tune it to a certain frequency and say 'I want to speak to Sponge-bag,' after which they would follow her instructions.

    By this time, I was at my little headquarters in a local farm, where a few of us were trying to keep abreast of who had reached where. The crucial contact, though, was with Sponge-bag — if they missed her, God knows where they would end up and we might never see them again. That night, I sat crouched over the radio in my farm, tuned to the same frequency, waiting in vain for the first escaper's call.

    After some hours, ghastly visions of hypothermic, hungry soldiers lost in the bogs of Bodmin Moor got the better of me and I lost my nerve. I had concealed a 'dead letter' in a tin by a clearing in a pine wood on the edge of Davidstow Moor airfield and assumed that either it was too well hidden or that someone had removed it. There seemed to be no alternative to flying back there and checking that all was well. Although the night was very dark and Bodmin Moor was a black hole without a light to be seen anywhere, I jumped into a Gazelle helicopter and flew off on my mission of mercy. This was long before the introduction of night vision equipment, so I relied on the naked eye and nothing else.

As I set off for the clearing, little alarm bells began to ring. It would be light again in three hours — surely I could wait that long? No, I couldn't. An approach to a small clearing in darkness without any approach aid and without a daylight reconnaissance was lunacy, surely? Maybe, I reasoned, but I had no alternative.

By the time I had arrived over where the tin was concealed, I settled down to the task of getting into the clearing without further ado. There was no time for a preliminary recce from the air and it was clearly a very tight fit but by altering the angle of the landing lamp so that I could approach down the beam picking out the floor of the clearing, I was able to drop slowly into place. Stopping the rotors but keeping the engine running (a starter failure in that situation being too awful to contemplate), I stepped out of the Gazelle, took a couple of paces and tripped headlong over an enormous felled tree trunk, breaking my torch in the process.

What followed was pure music hall as I stumbled about in the pitch darkness, cursing as I groped about for that blasted tin. To make matters worse, I was sure that there were escapers concealed nearby who were watching all this with barely stifled mirth. Quite rightly, they kept silent as the melodrama unfolded before them. Finally, by sheer luck I found the tin, which was still where I had planted it, making my whole trip absolutely pointless. However, weak with relief that the exercise was still on track, I walked back to the aircraft, tripped over the tree trunk a second time and more or less fell into the cockpit.

As I lifted from the clearing, I realised that that felled tree trunk, unseen as I approached to land, could have been the end of me and, for all I knew, others who were concealed nearby, if I had placed one of the aircraft's skids on it while landing.

It was a bruised and much chastened squadron commander who set course for the farm, tuned to that crucial frequency and finally heard that phrase he had been anticipating for so long:

'I want to speak to Sponge-bag!'

THE UNDIPLOMATIC BAG

Few Army Air Corps officers can expect to fly all the time and there are inevitably occasions when the powers that be decree a short spell on the staff. The real skill here is to ensure that it is the shortest spell possible, since few aviators actually enjoy staff work. By the time my squadron command tour came to an end, I had no cause to complain — indeed it might have been poetic justice if I had been sentenced to interminable tours on the staff from then onwards.

I had already served a two year sentence in the Main Building of the Ministry of Defence in Whitehall and swore that I would never *ever* go there again under *any* circumstances. So I suppose it was inevitable that I would be warned for a return to that particular hell hole in 1978.

The title of my new job was an acronym that meant nothing to me, except for the letters 'MA' which stand for Military Assistant — a sort of glorified bag-carrier for some great man, which was often regarded as a make-or-break appointment. Get it right and the sky was the limit to your career, but get it even slightly wrong and you would sink without trace. The notion that I would have to organise the day-to-day work of a very senior officer, when I couldn't even organise myself very effectively, turned my blood to ice. I was dreading it as I turned up for the first day in a job which actually turned out to be one of the most exciting I can remember.

The poor individual who landed Major Mallock as his MA was an Admiral and the senior serving intelligence man in the country. This scared me even more; I knew little about the Royal Navy and had never dabbled in the occult of intelligence in my life. He was steeped in it, however, and would clearly not need much help from me in that department, so long as his office and small team of staff worked smoothly. Moreover, he was an aviator himself with a distinguished record flying dive bombers off carriers in the Pacific war, so we hit it off right from the start.

I couldn't believe my luck. All my friends who had done time as MAs seemed to work for gimlet-eyed, ascetic bullies with short tempers who ate their staff for breakfast and thought nothing of putting in a fourteen-hour day in the London office. My Admiral couldn't have been more different. Small and dapper with a wide grin, he was modest, humorous and congenial. He came into the office at 9 and left at 5.30, except for Mondays when he started late and Fridays when he left early, so that he could enjoy his weekends at home with his wife.

He had been in the intelligence business so long that he knew what was important and what wasn't, so he didn't waste his time or mine. Furthermore, he took the view that I couldn't do my job properly unless I was cleared to the same security level as he was, and that I should travel with him in first class whenever he went on tour. I realised that working for him would be enormous fun and was determined to pull my socks up.

The intelligence material to which I was privy was truly terrifying. The West was being overtaken by Russia and the Warsaw Pact in just about every department and the news was getting worse every day. Politically, everything also seemed to be happening at once: the Iranian revolution, the Russian invasion of Afghanistan, problems in Cambodia, Vietnam and the Middle East — all had to be watched by our intelligence staff. Cleared to Top Secret codeword level, I was indoctrinated on arrival and left in no doubt what would happen if I allowed this information to fall into the wrong hands. I sometimes felt like putting my fingers in my ears to avoid hearing still more ghastly developments.

After a few weeks, however, the novelty wore off and the hard work began, although there were still amusing occasions to savour. As the Shah of Iran fought to stay on the peacock throne, I would read daily telegrams from Sir Anthony Parsons, our ambassador in Tehran, which read like a situation comedy. Monday's signal would read: *'I had an audience with his Serene Highness last night and thought he looked a little peaky.'* This was followed on Tuesday by: *'Spoke again to his Serene Highness yesterday and told him to keep his nerve. He seems to be confident that he can contain the situation.'*

Wednesday's communiqué was short but to the point: *'Went to the palace to see his Serene Highness last night. He wasn't there.'* The economy of expression by the Diplomatic Service is truly exemplary, for his Serene Highness had 'done a runner'!

The Admiral's previous posting had been as the head of the British Intelligence Staff in Washington and he was keen to visit his old friends and compare notes. He told me where he wanted to go and who to see and left me to sort out the itinerary. I was to accompany him and he wanted to take his Director of Service Intelligence, a Major General, along as well.

When it came to listing the topics which he wanted to discuss with his American opposite number, he made it clear that the usual practice of sending sensitive documents beforehand by diplomatic bag to the British Embassy was not convenient for him, since there was so much detail he had to absorb and he needed time to brief himself during the tour. I consulted the Foreign Office, where I was told that the only way this could be done officially was for me to become a diplomatic courier. This involved a morning at the Foreign Office in King Charles Street the day before departure, where I was briefed on how to conduct myself. The documents were closed with a lead seal in a diplomatic pouch, locked into a special security briefcase with the royal cipher on the flap and the case in turn was chained and locked round my wrist. It was a hellish feeling, knowing that I was as one with some of the most fearsome secrets in the government's possession, some of which were specifically *not* for the eyes of the Americans.

There were so many documents in the bag that it was a struggle to close and lock the flap of the briefcase. To help in accounting for them, I had a comprehensive list of them, on which I could check them out and back during our travels. On arrival in Washington, I handed the bag to the military Chief Clerk at the Embassy, where the Admiral and the General were both staying, while I booked into a hotel in downtown Rosslyn.

The first two days were spent in the Pentagon where, true to his word, the Admiral ensured that I was present at each presentation by the US Defence Intelligence Agency staff, during which I was asked to take notes. These were the men who briefed the President on the threat from behind the iron curtain and they all frightened me to death. The Russian submarines went faster and dived more deeply and silently than ours, their nuclear missiles had more warheads, greater range and accuracy, their tanks were tougher and more heavily armed, their aircraft were equipped with more sophisticated radar than ours, and so on. The litany was almost endless.

As we moved from place to place, the Admiral or General would ask for some specific document or other from my briefcase and I would hand it to him and make a mental note to retrieve it later. At the end of the day, the bulging briefcase would be returned to the Embassy for safekeeping overnight. On our first evening, the Pentagon hosted a cocktail party in the Watergate Hotel, which was nice, and the Admiral was due to entertain them all at a return match in the Embassy the following night. Since I had to return to my hotel to change after our day at the Pentagon, the Chief Clerk suggested that I should keep the briefcase until I could hand it over to him at the Embassy before the party started.

When I got back to my hotel, I had a quick shower and change and was waiting for a staff car to pick me up when I just happened to check the lock on the briefcase. It suddenly occurred to me that it seemed suspiciously easy to shut the flap before locking it. With feverish fingers and thumbs, I emptied the contents onto my bed to count up the documents.

There were two missing. Both were top secret and one was not under any circumstances to be released to the Americans.

Numb with foreboding on arrival at the Embassy with the briefcase, I told the Chief Clerk at once what the problem was. He blanched slightly, but said that the Pentagon were very good at 'sweeping' areas which had been visited and that they would probably return the documents promptly. This was cold comfort, in view of the contents of one of them. He said cheerfully 'Don't worry, sir. Enjoy the party and I'll let you know what I can find out.'

I have never enjoyed a cocktail party less. Every so often, I would catch sight of the Chief Clerk by the door, shaking his head sadly. Obviously, nothing had been found.

As the party broke up, the Chief Clerk suggested that I go back to my hotel for the night and he would ring my room first thing in the morning with the latest news, if any. I was due to make my own way to the CIA Headquarters in Langley, where the Admiral and General planned to meet me before spending the day with the 'spooks'. If nothing had turned up by then, there would be no alternative to falling on my sword.

After a totally sleepless night in the Holiday Inn in Rosslyn, I was informed by the Chief Clerk that he had drawn a blank. There was nothing for it — when we met up at Langley, I would have to tell the Admiral what had happened and I would then fly back to London alone to face the music and help try to limit the damage. The Chief Clerk had had the foresight to check that a seat in economy class was available between Dulles Airport and Heathrow the next day.

I found myself chained to that wretched briefcase on the steps of the CIA building the following morning. To add insult to injury, it was a beautiful, warm day with the trees in all their autumn glory. A limousine finally drew up at the foot of the steps and the Admiral and General got out and headed up towards me. My military career now at its end, I stepped forward and saluted.

'Admiral, there's something...' I began but he smiled and, unzipping a slim leather folder which he always kept with him on his travels, he handed me two buff envelopes.

'Good morning, Ross,' he said, adding casually 'I think you had better keep these. I've finished with them for the time being and I don't think we'll need them today but it's as well to have them handy.'

The look in his eyes as I took those missing documents from him was impenetrable, but I was sure that he knew well enough what I had been through.

He never mentioned the matter again and in his wisdom obviously considered that the torment that I had suffered was lesson enough for the future.

Some lessons, perhaps, are best learned the hard way.

A LONG DAY'S NIGHT

For any Army pilot in Germany, the airfield outside the Westphalia town of Detmold became something of a hub of one's existence. It came as a relief to me in 1980 that, lucky though I was to be given a regiment to command, it would be one of the two Army Air Corps regiments stationed in Detmold.

Hobart Barracks, where we lived, had a diverse population which made for an enjoyable social life. Perversely, my regiment worked directly to the Corps Headquarters up the road in Bielefeld and therefore had no operational responsibility for the Armoured Brigade headquarters on my Detmold doorstep. Administratively, however, the local Brigade Commander doubled as my garrison boss, responsible for discipline and the working of the military estate in which my regiment was established. Despite its complication, this tortuous arrangement seemed to work well enough.

One of the Garrison Commander's duties was to conduct what was then known as my Annual Review of the Unit, or ARU. There appeared to be no standard form of an ARU, since it depended on the whim of the commander and staff who carried it out, but it usually included a check on physical fitness, chemical warfare defence, small arms firing and low level tactics over the course of a day's work.

Brigadier James Stephenson, the new Garrison Commander, was a large, garrulous individual who clearly relished his progression up the greasy pole. On the whole, we got on well but I found he was all too ready to criticise the Army Air Corps for some perceived weakness or other in military knowledge. Whenever he held a conference involving all his commanding officers and staff, he seldom missed the chance to ridicule 'the light blue beret' for some oversight or other.

'You people who wear the light blue beret ought to spend less time flying about and more time doing some proper soldiering — you know, digging defensive positions, night patrolling and so on' he would say. God knows I'd heard it all before, usually from senior officers who had applied unsuccessfully in their youth to train as pilots themselves and thereafter lost no chance to get their own back on the system. As it happened, my regiment contained a large number of ex-infantrymen and others, who were highly experienced as conventional soldiers, and I'm glad to say that the opportunity finally came my way to show the great man what they could do.

It was the great man himself who gave me the opening, when he rang me to ask what I would like to do for my regiment's Annual Review. I suggested that, rather then set up the usual sideshow of fitness and skill at arms tests, he should accompany us into the field as a complete regiment over a night and a day and see for himself how we went about our business.

'I'll be bringing my two senior staff officers with me,' he said. 'Where shall we meet and when?'

We agreed a date and I suggested that he and his two majors should meet me outside the hangar at 11 o'clock at night, 'So that we can do some night patrolling and so on.' I said. There was a snort at the other end of the line but he agreed.

When the day dawned, the whole regiment moved out of barracks with all its aircraft and vehicles to take up positions in what were then known as emergency survival areas: places which had been prepared for occupation at short notice in the event of a Soviet invasion across the East German border. Only one helicopter was left behind: a solitary

Gazelle in which I was to transport the brigadier and his staff into the undergrowth in the dark that night.

And dark it certainly was as I waited for my passengers — no moon or stars, an overcast, warm night with the threat of rain later. The posse turned up as arranged, clambered into the Gazelle, strapped in and away we went. Our first port of call was to be 669 Squadron's position some twenty miles east of Detmold, where they had had all day to dig in and prepare for the visit. All was very quiet in my aircraft as the Brigadier and his henchmen strained to see where we were going in the enveloping blackness. Occupation of survival areas was always carried out under radio silence, so even the comforting chatter of the command radio net was denied us. This was probably the first time my passengers had ever flown in a helicopter at night. The Gazelle was not fitted with any navigation aid or night vision equipment in those days, so all night flying had to be done on dead reckoning. 669 Squadron's position was miles from any habitation, there was not a light to be seen below us anywhere and my passengers began to enquire nervously what I intended to do.

After ten minutes, I was just beginning to wonder myself, when without warning two sets of stationary converging Land Rover headlights were switched on directly beneath us. Turning into wind and descending onto final approach, we landed in the pool of light, switched off the engine and the lights were extinguished again.

Everybody in the regiment had been briefed to ensure that our three visitors had no time to draw breath, so they were collected and spirited away into the darkness to tour the Squadron position before the next phase of the exercise. Apart from meals and the occasional cup of tea, they were to remain on the move without a break, either on the ground or in the air.

By daybreak, they were beginning to look a bit worse for wear, having accompanied foot patrols through the night, but they bravely battled on through an assault on a defended bridge during the morning, regularly taking the air individually to watch phases of the operation from above. Lunch was served by 659 Squadron in some style, allowing their sore feet to recover somewhat, at which point the Brigadier suddenly announced that he wanted me to move my regiment as soon as possible to a position which his Chief of Staff would give me when we were airborne again. I was ready for this, knowing how much the Brigadier liked to throw surprises in all directions. However, if there was one thing I was absolutely sure about, it was the ability of my Adjutant to issue timely and accurate movement instructions to everybody and, as we climbed away in our Gazelle, I heard him on the radio giving warning orders to all concerned.

My original Gazelle had developed a fault, so had been replaced with another at the last moment. The new one had been fitted with dual controls, so I asked the brigadier if he would mind sitting in the back seat with his Chief of Staff, where he would not be at risk of inadvertently disturbing the flying controls.

'God, what a silly fuss!' he said, getting yet again into his 'light blue beret' form. 'Why can't you chaps give us credit for some intelligence for once? To hell with your rules, I'm going to travel in the front as usual. I won't touch anything.'

I should have dug my heels in, since passengers were not allowed to occupy the front seat with dual controls fitted, but the day had gone well and I didn't want to spoil it with a pointless argument. Once airborne, I opened the piece of paper the Chief of Staff had given me and found to my horror that the grid reference he had written down was just off my map. Horror turned to bemusement when I realised that he was actually sending us off into East Germany. The Brigadier saw my expression of surprise and chuckled.

I was completely baffled. A complex and comprehensive system of surveillance of air traffic in the area of the border was backed up by NATO air defence, including missiles and Quick Reaction Alert fighters — and that was just on our side. The rules of engagement were absolute and certainly no exception would be entertained in the event of an illegal crossing by a British Army helicopter.

'Forgive me, Brigadier, but are you absolutely *sure* you want to go to this grid reference?' I asked.

He grinned. 'Absolutely.'

His grin faded as he looked at the direction indicator on the instrument panel.

'What the hell are we going this way for?' he asked.

'Because' I said, 'You want 9 Regiment Army Air Corps to move to Magdeburg, Brigadier!'

'For Christ's sake turn round!' he yelped, although we actually had some way to go before we were likely to be intercepted.

'Give me that!' he added, snatching the piece of paper and comparing the grid reference with his map.

'Chief of Staff,' he said to the hapless major in the rear seat, 'You're a blithering idiot. You've got those figures the wrong way round.'

He turned back to me sheepishly.

'We're meant to be going to Sennelager' he said, lamely. Sennelager was a training area just a few miles west of where we had started in Detmold. It seemed a rather prosaic end to what might have been quite an adventure!

It had been raining hard for some time as we arrived on Sennelager ranges but that hadn't stopped these 'light blue berets' from digging down half way to Australia. It was actually quite difficult to find all the regiment's positions; the aircraft and vehicles had been camouflaged so heavily, everybody had dug a personal slit trench and were hard at work improving them in the pouring rain.

We landed alongside a Sergeant air crewman, digging as if his life depended on it. The Brigadier didn't wait for me to throttle back the engine and opened his door as the Sergeant snapped him a salute which would have done credit to the Brigade of Guards in which he had originally served.

'I think we'll call a halt here,' said the Brigadier to me before he disconnected his headset, 'But I'd just like a word with this very smart young NCO.'

So saying, he leapt out of the aircraft, catching the heel of his boot on the dual collective lever. The Gazelle jumped two feet into the air before I could gather my wits, as the Brigadier clung to the open door with one foot on the port skid. I landed and closed the throttle quickly as the Sergeant, now ashen-faced, saluted for a second time...

All we had to do now was return to Detmold and, as the dual controls were discreetly removed by the REME, I briefed the pilots for an 18-aircraft formation flight home. On this occasion I gave the lead of the formation to one of the squadron commanders, so that I could fly the Brigadier at the back, to give him a good view.

He was very quiet as we flew home on the outside of a 'Vic' of Gazelles. I assumed his silence was the result of his natural embarrassment at nearly causing a serious accident but, as I looked across at him, I realised with a jolt that he was feeling horribly airsick. There was nothing I could do to make him more comfortable and I realised, too late as usual, that I had no idea if a sick-bag was stowed anywhere within reach.

Slowly we approached the airfield as he turned increasingly green round the gills. He gave a faint groan as we changed formation into line astern before running in over the runway for a break to land. Not wishing to subject him to the indignity of clearing up his own lunch, I banked very gently and as we landed, colour slowly returned to his unshaven cheeks.

The poor chap had been on the go for eighteen hours, with no sleep and scarcely any rest, but he perked up as I stopped the engine.

'Ross, tell them all to gather round. I want to say a few words.'

The aircrew collected by my aircraft, as Brigadier James Stephenson OBE gave a short but highly complimentary debrief on their performance during their exercise. I felt enormously proud of them as he admitted that he had not fully appreciated the complexity and hazards of what they did for a living, and how impressed he was at their obvious expertise.

'One last point,' he said. 'Whatever you do, don't run yourselves down.'

Coming from the lips of a man who had constantly 'run us down' whenever he got the chance, I thought that was a bit rich.

'You are as good, if not better, than anyone else in this garrison' he continued. 'You have every reason to be proud of yourselves.'

Perhaps it was my imagination, but thereafter the Garrison Commander seemed to spend less of his time being rude about 'the light blue beret'.

THE PERSONAL TOUCH

I was still serving in Germany when the Army Air Corps celebrated its silver jubilee in 1982. The central event of this affair was an enormous international air show at Middle Wallop and, like most members of the tribe, I was keen to get back to England to enjoy some of the festivities and meet some old friends.

I managed to wangle a trip back to England in a German Army helicopter — one of their 'Jolly Green Giant' CH-53s, which was stuffed to the gunwales with hitch hikers like me. It was due to fly as part of the air show and the Germans, with unimpeachable logic, thought that it would be a waste to fly out and back with just its own crew on board. This was just as well, because the Brits in Germany were facing bankruptcy again and self-drive by helicopter was forbidden.

I had booked into the Officers' Mess for the long weekend. I had heard that there were plans afoot to demolish the historic old accommodation huts behind the Officers' Mess, where I had spent the first year of my time as a flying student, but was relieved that they not only still stood but were pressed into service to accommodate overseas visitors for the occasion. Furthermore, I was allotted the same room in the same hut as I had originally occupied eighteen years earlier. Apart from the odd lick of paint here and there, little had changed in the meantime, except that now Mrs Ruston was no longer on duty as my batwoman. I assumed that she had retired or moved elsewhere and regretted the fact that we were not going to meet again after so long.

'Rusty' could do no wrong in my eyes. For the eleven months that I had occupied that room in 1964-65, Rusty's unobtrusive presence lent a certain routine and stability to my bachelor existence, from the moment she produced a cup of tea to rouse me in the morning to her departure for home at five o'clock with a cheery goodbye. Springing out of bed to greet the dawn has never been my strong point, so the need to be at morning briefing on the airfield at 8 o'clock for an 8.30 take-off meant a 7 o'clock reveille, which Rusty never missed. Cleaning, laundry, encouragement and the occasional discreet rocket — Rusty did everything with quiet good humour and real style.

On the morning of the air show, I had some time to kill, so called on Trubshaw, my old friend and colleague from the Blue Eagle days, who had retired from the Army to a civil aviation job and lived in a house at Cholderton nearby. Out of the blue, he mentioned the sad news that Rusty's husband had just died and that she was on compassionate leave from work in the Mess. Trubshaw being Trubshaw, he knew where Rusty's house was and suggested that we should call on her and offer our condolences.

Off we set in Trubshaw's little Morris Minor. Rusty's house was on the outskirts of Andover, from where she would cycle the four miles into work every morning. When we arrived, we were relieved to see that her family were all there with her and that she was coping well with her bereavement. Nonetheless, she insisted on making us a cup of tea and we stayed for a good chat. She apologised that she was not working that weekend but hoped that I understood the situation. We spent a short time reminiscing about what life had been like in the 1960s, how things had changed since and had some laughs about some mutual friends who had been her charges after my time in her tender care. When we left she was her cheerful, stoic self, clearly well supported by her extended family.

The air show was a splendid affair and the day ended with a dinner in the Officers' Mess, which seemed to go on for most of the night. In those days, Rusty and all the Mess staff were directly employed by the Ministry of Defence, most of them serving for many years. Our single Officers' Mess gardener, for example, had started work there in 1944 and there were many who had worked continuously for twenty years or more. As a result of this, the ethos of the Mess staff was to 'see the job through', no matter how long it took. There was never any question of stopping a party early to save staff wages and, no matter how long the carousing continued, the Mess would be buffed up and back to normal by breakfast time. It was almost a form of witchcraft.

I waddled my way back to my little hut at about four o'clock in the morning, without a care in the world apart from the threat of the nuclear hangover to come at daybreak. No matter — the Germans were probably just as late to bed, so we were unlikely to leave for home much before teatime.

At seven o'clock, I was suddenly aware of that familiar sound of a teacup and saucer being placed quietly on my bedside table, followed by a gentle shaking of my shoulder.

'It's seven o'clock, sir,' said a familiar voice. 'You'll be flying today, I imagine.'

As I prised open my bloodshot eyes, Rusty's face swam into view. She smiled.

'Thought you might like a cuppa. Just for old time's sake.' she said.

It had a dash of milk and one sugar — just the way I like it.

THE ASHES

In 1988, my last appointment in Army flying was one which I had dreamed of but never thought would be mine — in command of the Army Air Corps Centre at Middle Wallop. The job attracted a 'tied cottage' of some style. No 1 Falaise Road was originally built as one of two RAF Group Captains' quarters when the airfield was laid out as a potential bomber station in the 1930s, to an architectural plan designed by Edwin Lutyens.

When I was learning to fly at Middle Wallop twenty-four years earlier, it had housed the Brigadier. Now I was to have the run of the place myself with its six bedrooms. Having passed from RAF to Army ownership in 1957, 1 Falaise Road had inevitably suffered from the usual neglect lavished on its estate by an impoverished Army which regularly raided the property maintenance budget when it couldn't make ends meet. No matter — ignoring the dilapidation of the place, our teenaged offspring took over the top of the three floors and we gently expanded to fill the considerable room the house afforded.

My parishioners were responsible for training all Army pilots, aircrewmen and ground crew, all Army aircraft engineers and technicians, and for preparing Army Air Corps officers and soldiers for promotion. The airfield included a Logistics centre, an Aircraft Workshop and a rapidly-expanding Museum. And buried within this catholic population was a treasure trove of sixty-eight aircraft of eight different types. I was in my element.

Mercifully, although I was given a budget to finance what we did, the modern fixation with money and accountancy had not yet become a component part of the military ethos, so I was able to ignore it in my day-to-day running of the place and leave accountancy to my hard-pressed but amiable budget manager.

The great thing was that I was able to fly whenever I had a spare moment. Furthermore, the aircraft at Middle Wallop were operated by friends who were happy to let me indulge myself as long as I didn't intrude too much into their affairs. After a quick check of the diary first thing in the morning, all I had to do was ring somebody up to see if an aircraft was spare for a spell that day and book it. This system worked very well, and incidentally ensured that I was away from the telephone for long periods, which I have always found a godsend. After a while, people who want to consult you on all sorts of ghastly little technicalities get fed up with waiting for an answer, sort the matter out themselves and leave you alone.

One particular perk of the job was a full-time staff car driver. I had last enjoyed such a luxury as a Commanding officer in Germany and I was well aware what a thankless job that of a staff car driver can be. In order to mitigate the boredom of waiting around to be called to go somewhere at a moment's notice, I developed the habit of taking my driver flying with me, which seemed a fair exchange of scene. All the Middle Wallop training aircraft were equipped with dual controls, so it was a simple matter to indulge in a little flying instruction from time to time, although this would probably have been frowned upon if it was known in official circles.

One driver in particular took to this treatment like a duck to water. Lance Corporal Graham Wayman drove my staff car like Lewis Hamilton but clearly had a natural enthusiasm for flying, whether inverted in a Chipmunk or dashing between the trees in a Gazelle. I developed a suspicion that he would make a better pilot than a driver and, in the long run, I was to be proved right.

One of the cardinal rules in aviation is to have a specific aim in mind before take off. The pilot who leaves the ground without a firm idea of what is to be achieved is a menace to himself and others. Wayman's delight in getting airborne was a tonic and we would spend hours honing his skills in low level map reading, with a bit of pure flying training from time to time. Indeed, there came a time when I dearly wished to have an hour or so on my own practising aerobatics in a Chipmunk and cunningly managed to slip away from the office without his knowledge, while he was away refuelling the staff car. Alas, he found out about this and, just as I was about to taxi away towards the runway, I felt the aircraft rock slightly as Wayman dropped into the rear seat and buckled himself in.

'Sorry I'm late, sir,' he said over the intercom, 'I didn't realise you were planning to get airborne.'

There was even the odd occasion when I could be of use. An institution as large as the Army Air Corps Centre was constantly approached by the media, charities and other agencies for help and it was often possible to combine a little good work with the Commandant's irritating desire to fly. I recall with amazement the spectacle of the start of the Whitbread Round the World Race in the Solent, when a BBC camera crew in the back of my Lynx was able to broadcast close-up pictures of the Army's yacht (skippered by an ex Chief Flying Instructor) as the sea was churned into turmoil by thousands of boats of all shapes and sizes.

Sadly, there were a number of appeals from parents to grant the dying wishes of their seriously ill offspring by giving them a helicopter trip. What always struck me about these passengers was the extraordinary gratitude they expressed for what was such a short and simple favour, which we were fortunate enough to be in a position to grant. One small girl from Winchester, Helen Carlick, aged twelve, was recovering from treatment of a brain tumour and was so thin that it was difficult to secure her properly in the front seat. We flew in a Gazelle around Salisbury Plain on a bright and warm summer's day and she spent most of the sortie singing lustily at the top of her lungs. She died three months later and Winchester Cathedral was thronged at her funeral.

The Director of the Museum of Army Flying at this time was Colonel Michael Hickey. Michael was a military historian who knew an enormous number of retired Army aviators and occasionally asked if I could help bereaved families, where the deceased had asked for his ashes to be scattered over the airfield. We soon put together a small informal ceremony which was simple to set up and much appreciated by those involved. Inevitably, it took place in the early evening when training had finished, most of the staff had returned home and I had reached the bottom of my in-tray in the Commandant's office.

The family and friends would congregate for a short service in the chapel behind my headquarters. At the end, I would meet them in my flying suit and they would hand over the urn of ashes. As I headed off to join my driver at the waiting Gazelle, the family would move to the impressive war memorial at the bottom of the entrance road to the airfield, where they would await the arrival of the helicopter overhead. Wayman and I would fly slowly down the road from the main gate, pass over the family by the memorial and descend onto the grass of the airfield, where the ashes would be scattered out of sight of the mourners. It was a dignified, simple and rather moving ritual, cost the exchequer virtually nothing and was greatly appreciated by those who attended. Corporal Wayman and I did a number of these little ceremonies and it was nice to feel that we were contributing something to the regimental family in the process.

It only went wrong once. The evening was warm and still and, by six o'clock, silence had descended on the airfield. The little group in the chapel greeted me warmly and handed over the urn containing the ashes. It had a screw top, rather like a thermos flask. After a short chat, I set off for the aircraft which, in view of the warm weather, had had its front doors removed. In no time at all, Wayman and I were airborne, curving over the Museum to line up with the main entrance to the airfield at about a hundred feet.

Slowing down to about 50 knots, I spotted the little group of people by the war memorial. All was is it should have been, so I warned Wayman to prepare to scatter the ashes just as soon as we had completed the fly past.

There was a short pause.

'Christ!' said my driver, 'I can't get the top off!'

Looking across the cockpit, I could see his face was crimson with the effort of unscrewing the lid. We were now approaching the main gates, the upturned faces plain to see. I slowed down even more. By this time, Wayman had become pretty good at flying the Gazelle, so I handed control to him as I struggled with the wretched urn myself. The lid still wouldn't budge.

Looking back, I can see now that there was really no drama in the situation at all. The family by the memorial had no idea of our predicament and all we had to do was fly over them, descend onto the grass out of their field of view and sort the problem out in our own time. But it didn't seem like this at the time. Swept up by the gravitas of the situation, it became absolutely vital to get the top off that blasted urn before it was too late. I flew the aircraft more and more slowly as we passed the mourners, Graham Wayman grunting and swearing as he strained at the lid.

Finally, as I brought the Gazelle gently to the hover over the airfield, Wayman yelled 'Got it!', tore off the lid and shook the ashes out onto the grass outside. Unfortunately, the downdraught from the main rotor caught them and blasted them in a dense cloud in all directions. Coughing and spluttering, we taxied slowly back to the hangar, our faces and the inside of the aircraft coated in a thick layer of grey ash.

As the ground crewman walked towards us with the ground handling wheels, preparing to drag the aircraft into its hangar for the night, he gave a quick glance round the inside of the aircraft.

'Hmmm,' he muttered, 'Going to need the Hoover tonight, I reckon.'

As I handed back the empty urn to the family, I could see that they had been moved by the occasion. In the circumstances, how could I admit that their loved one now nestled inside a vacuum cleaner in Hangar 4?